STICKY LEADERSHIP AND MANAGEMENT

LEAD WITH INTEGRITY AND MANAGE WITH
CONFIDENCE

STICKY SERIES
BOOK 3

PETER LYLE DEHAAN, PHD

ROCK ROOSTER BOOKS

ISBN

- 979-8-88809-069-5 (e-book)
- 979-8-88809-070-1 (paperback)
- 979-8-88809-071-8 (hardcover)
- 979-8-88809-072-5 (audiobook)

Library of Congress Control Number: 9798888090701

Published by Rock Rooster Books, Grand Rapids, Michigan

Credits

- Developmental editor: Julie Harbison
- Copy editor: Robyn Mulder
- Cover design: Taryn Nergaard
- Author photo: Jordan Leigh Photography

The stories in this book are all true, as I remember them. I did, however, change some names and inconsequential details.

To all who lead and manage others

CONTENTS

LEADERSHIP AND MANAGEMENT

Lead with Effectiveness and Manage with Confidence

Leadership is the ability to cast a vision and draw others to you in a collective pursuit of that vision. The mark of leadership, therefore, is if you have followers. And the mark of *great* leadership is if you have *committed* followers. Conversely, someone with no followers is not a leader.

Early in my life, I'd often hear people say I was a natural born leader. I was never sure why they said this, and their conviction perplexed me.

In retrospect, it was my attitude. I told my peers

what to do and expected them to comply. Usually they did.

Many an esteemed leader, I understand, is either a firstborn or an only child. This family dynamic predisposes children to develop leadership capabilities—or at least leadership attitudes. My leadership characteristics may have resulted from being a firstborn. And since my sister followed me by seven years, I also had most of the characteristics of an only child. In this respect, my birth order predisposed me toward leadership.

In looking over my career and my life, I see times of leadership success but also times of leadership failure. Though every leader experiences times when things don't go as expected, my shortfalls grated on me. Each one caused me to question my leadership ability.

Most of my leadership successes came in the field of business. My followers were my employees. At the risk of oversimplification, I paid them to follow me. Yes, some did so with a sold-out commitment to the vision we pursued, while others did so with lesser enthusiasm. I suspect the paycheck—and not my charisma or "natural leadership ability"—was why they followed me.

Outside the business realm, be it in industry organizations or nonprofits, my leadership outcomes produced satisfaction as well as frustration. Yes, I excelled at leading writing critique groups and Bible studies, but opportunities of a larger scope sometimes provided greater challenges.

In all those cases, there was no employment component, so followers held an interest in a shared vision or desired outcome. And it was my appeal and effectiveness as a leader that either drew them in or caused them to retreat.

Yet, concurrent to this, I also worked at becoming a humble leader, one with less swagger. I knew how to be a cocky leader, but how to lead with humility too often escaped me, even though I knew it was possible.

Parallel to this, I also had management potential. Contrary to my leadership promise, I saw my propensity for management from an early age. This skill—along with intentional development along the way—resulted in a lifelong string of management successes. At least that's how I see them. And for those few years when I wasn't in management, I chafed at the shortcomings of my superiors. I was sure they were doing it wrong.

Management is the ability to analyze a situation —such as staffing, infrastructure, finances, operations, or customer service—to determine the best course of action to move forward and accomplish the desired outcome. With a plan in place, managers implement it, all the while adjusting to produce the best results in the shortest amount of time.

Management success requires an analytical mindset, which is a skill I see in myself.

Leadership and management connect. Though sometimes a situation is clearly leadership or clearly management, usually there is no obvious dividing line between the two, with successful leadership giving way to management and successful management tapping into leadership. They exist on a continuum. In truth, most situations require leaders to also manage and managers to also lead.

Therefore, I'll treat the two concepts as interchangeable, all the while knowing that not all leaders are managers and not all managers are leaders. Yet, I maintain that the best ones are both.

If you see yourself as a leader but not a manager, or a manager but not a leader, don't despair. Instead of trying to be what you aren't, celebrate what you are and align yourself with someone who possesses the skills you lack.

Regardless of your situation or where you see yourself on the leadership-management continuum, this book is for you. Seize its lessons to lead with more effectiveness and manage with greater success, all the while doing so with integrity and excellence.

THE POWER OF A COMPLIMENT

Telling Others You Appreciate Them Makes a Huge Difference

In the years between high school graduation and my first proper job, I took on a variety of part-time work while being a full-time student. One position was an audio engineer at a TV station.

After an awkward interview, Stan—the current audio engineer—hired me because I could start the next day.

The first day I listened and watched Stan work. As he explained it, the job seemed simple. There was lots of idle time, four live broadcasts and, on some days, production work in between. He was more interested, however, in regaling me with his glory days as a radio DJ than in training me. It turned out that Stan was also a silent partner in an out-of-town enterprise. He needed to be actively involved to protect his investment. At the end of my two weeks of training, Stan would leave.

On my second day, Stan let me touch the control panel, and I did the first live segment. It was a 30-second weather report. I turned on the mike for the weatherman when the director cued him and turned it off at the end of the segment. I did a mike check beforehand and monitored the audio level during the broadcast. A half hour later, I did the second live broadcast, too, a one-minute news segment. Stan did the third segment. It had two mikes, one for news and the other for weather.

The half-hour noon show, however, overwhelmed me. There were half a dozen mikes to activate, monitor, and turn off; recordings for musical bridges; an array of audio sources; and a live announcer. There was also an abrupt change in plans if a segment ran long or if there was time to fill.

On the third day, Stan called in to tell me he would be late. He reviewed expectations of the first two segments, and I did them solo. He called later, before the third, and we talked it through. Stan promised to be in before the noon show.

I did the third segment by myself.

Stan called to say he had been watching, and I had done fine. Could I do the noon show by myself?

"No!" I asserted.

"Okay," he assured, "I'll come in, but let's talk through it just in case." I never saw Stan again. My *training* was over.

With sweaty palms and a knotted gut, I muddled my way through the noon show, knowing that thousands would hear any miscue. By the time the show ended, I was physically exhausted. My head throbbed.

This pattern repeated itself with each noon show for the next several months. If only I had received more instruction.

On-the-job training was fine for production work. Time was not an issue, and retakes were common, expected, and accepted. If I lacked training in some area, the director coached me.

The live shows, however, were a different story. It was tense and nerve-racking. They expected perfection and didn't tolerate errors. This produced an incredible amount of pressure.

This stress was partly because of my lack of training, but more importantly a result of the directors. I worked with three. My favorite was kind. He remembered what it was like to do my job and was sympathetic. Unfortunately, I seldom worked with him.

The second director was aloof and focused only on the broadcast, not caring what he said or how he treated others. Fortunately, I didn't work with him too much.

Most of my interaction was with a third director. During live broadcasts, he became verbally volatile. He yelled a lot. When he was mad, he yelled louder —all laced with expletives. Management by intimidation was his style. My goal was to get through the noon show without receiving a verbal tongue-lashing. I wasn't always successful. Of course, this made me even more tense.

Although most of the work was fine, my angst from this half hour each day caused me to despise my job. Thankfully, my remaining time was short, as graduation neared. I grabbed the first job offer I could and gave my two-weeks' notice.

Ironically, the day after I submitted my resignation, the volatile director asked, "You should get some vacation soon, shouldn't you?"

"I haven't put in enough time yet," I replied. "Besides, I just gave my two-weeks' notice."

"What?" He slammed some papers on the table with a curse. "I can't believe it." His face turned red. "We finally get someone good, and they don't pay him enough to stay."

"Good?" I questioned. "I'm not good."

"You're the best audio engineer we've had in years."

"What about Stan?" I asked.

"Stan was always making mistakes. We couldn't get through a broadcast without him screwing it up. You did better your first week than he ever did."

"But I make mistakes all the time."

"They're trivial," he said with a dismissive wave of his hand. "Viewers don't even notice."

As he picked up his papers and left the room, I contemplated what he'd said. *I am good!*

Not surprisingly, I had a new attitude during the noon show that day. My nervousness dissipated. I made no mistakes, no one yelled at me, and most significantly, I enjoyed it. My job had become fun.

On my second to last day there, I met the weekend audio engineer. She was considering taking over my shift. She wanted to see what was involved in the noon show. Unfortunately, that day the show was the most difficult one I had ever encountered. There was a live band, with each person and instrument separately miked, plus there were a few unusual twists. I would need every piece of gear in the room and use the entire audio console. Although it was stressful, it was a good stress, because I was a good audio engineer. I performed my part without error, earning a rare compliment from my critical director. At the end of the show, I leaned back with the pride of a job well done.

My protégé shook her head. "I could never do that," she sighed, and left the room.

My last two weeks at the TV station were most enjoyable. As such, it is with fondness that I recall my time there.

How might things have been even better if someone had told me sooner that I was doing a good job?

Leadership and Management Success Tip

Remember to compliment staff and let them know when they excel—and not just when they fall short.

SOLICIT FEEDBACK FROM YOUR FRONTLINE STAFF

Verify Key Information and Don't Assume You Know the Answer

M y first full-time job was repairing copy machines. One day, toward the end of my short tenure there, the new service manager shared his vision for the future of the department. The company had two product lines, each with its own technical staff. This was inefficient, as the paths of the respective service teams would often overlap. His idea was to cross-train us on both product lines. Then we'd do less driving and be more efficient. Customers would receive quicker service, and the company would save money.

It was a clever idea, but I pointed out something he had overlooked. Already jammed with copy machine parts, my service vehicle had no room left to carry additional supplies for another product line. In fact, I had removed my spare tire to make room for the parts I needed to carry.

His once-pleased smile evaporated. My revelation, shooting down his brilliant idea, left him dismayed. I'm not sure if I was the first technician he shared his plan with, but I was the first one to point out why it wouldn't work.

I respected him as a leader, in part because he once did what I and my three dozen compatriots were doing now. But things had changed, with more models to service and more spare parts to carry. His assumption that his knowledge from years ago still applied today left him vulnerable to miscalculation.

This error can happen in any operation. Many people in management and leadership rose through the ranks, having done frontline work themselves. But things change over time, and what may have once made sense no longer applies.

That's why it's important for leaders to stay connected with what their frontline staff does each day. This doesn't mean having a vague comprehension, but instead possessing an in-depth under-standing.

Short of periodically doing your subordinates' work—which is a great idea—the solution is to talk with your frontline staff. This will help you better understand what they do on a day-to-day basis and support you in making informed decisions about the work they do and the policies you implement.

Leadership and Management Success Tip

Don't assume you know the answer to every problem. Seek feedback from staff. They'll either confirm or correct your perspective. Either way it's a win.

HOW TO BEST DEAL WITH CHANGE

Wise Leaders Understand Change and Know How to Navigate It

C hange happens. And the rate of change is accelerating. We experience change at home, at work, and in our community. When considering change, there are three general truths: change is opposed, change is viewed as loss, and change is mourned.

Change Is Opposed: Change represents a deviation from the status quo, from what's expected, whether good or bad. Change represents moving from the known to the unknown. Therefore, it's normal that people will oppose change and resist it to whatever degree they can.

This might mean clinging to the old ways, lobbying against change, or rebelling by acting out. They could offer resistance or exhibit passive-aggressive behavior.

Change Is Loss: All change means giving up something—even if it's something bad. Many people view change as a zero-sum game, which implies that there are winners and losers. When things change, they assume someone else must have won and, therefore, they lost. This assumption is natural when the change is not their idea.

Change Is Mourned: When something is lost, that loss is lamented. Sometimes the loss is perceived (it didn't happen) or potential (it might happen), whereas at other times it's real (it happened).

Regardless, the emotional reaction to loss is mourning. Just as there are steps to grieving, mourning the loss wrought by change will progressively proceed down a similar path.

Change Management

These common realities of change, however, aren't inevitable.

People can accept change if it's understood, occurs in small increments, and is within the control of those affected by it. This trio of suggestions may not offer much relief when we're confronted with global or national upheaval foisted upon us, because those situations are not within our control, nor do they occur in small doses—though we can seek to understand them.

But this advice is helpful when responding to changes in our lives—like children marrying and moving on—or work situations such as layoffs, job cuts, restructuring, office closings, wage freezes, or pay cuts.

In these circumstances, we can make a reasonable and successful effort to accept and even embrace change:

Change That Is Understood: We can best accept and deal with change if we understand it. This doesn't mean we need to agree with the reasons for the change, merely that we comprehend the decision to change.

Change in Small Increments: Change made over time and in small doses has a much better chance of acceptance and becomes more manageable. This gives time for a change to sink in and for people to adjust mentally and emotionally as the change transpires.

Change within Control of Those Affected by It: Whenever people can experience some control over a change, they're more likely to handle it positively. Providing options is significant, as is allowing people to have some input into how the change occurs.

Change Leadership

A final consideration is for those who decide for change. Yes, many will oppose it, view it as loss, and mourn it. But leaders can work to minimize or even negate those responses by communicating the reasons for the change, making small increments over time, and providing as much control as possible to those affected by it.

In the end, we might not escape change, but we can ease some of the negative reactions to it. This is how to succeed in dealing with change.

Leadership and Management Success Tip

Understand the truths about change to smartly manage it and wisely lead others through it.

LEADING A NONPROFIT BOARD OF DIRECTORS

Followers Must Be Willing and Able

I once volunteered for a local parachurch organization. They addressed an unmet need in our area, and I relished the chance to give back to my community.

It wasn't long before the executive director asked me to join the board of directors. I jumped at the opportunity, but what I experienced at my first meeting shocked me. Though the board members were willing, they lacked the ability to do what they were supposed to do. I earlier said that a leader must have followers. Let me amend that to say a leader must have *able* followers.

No one on the board understood what their role was or even knew what they were supposed to do. This included the board president, who struggled to run the meeting. For the better part of an hour, they discussed an ongoing fundraising effort that in good months brought in $25. Then they segued into a seasonal fundraising effort that produced even less. That was the extent of the meeting. *What have I gotten myself into?*

At my second meeting, they appointed me to fill the open vice president position. I agreed, seeing it as an opportunity to bring needed structure to a dysfunctional board.

Before the next meeting occurred, the board president resigned. The remaining board appointed me president at my third meeting.

Though everyone on the board was passionate about the group's mission, they all functioned better at the grassroots level and not at the board level.

Working with what I had, I set about reforming our meetings by introducing structure. Some board members welcomed my efforts and eagerly supported me. Other board members resisted my changes to the status quo and eventually resigned. Even so, some dissenters remained.

I worked at bringing higher-functioning volunteers onto the board. This raised the level of our discussions and improved our decision-making process, albeit not as much as I would have liked had I been able to find experienced board members.

One new board member, however, stood out. He was a businessman. We shared common ideals for how the organization should function and how to run meetings. At my suggestion, the board appointed him as vice president, and I groomed him to take over when my term ended.

Though the organization didn't yet have the board it deserved, I did turn the ship around. I got it moving in the right direction and at a decent speed.

I set my vice president up for success when he would take over the reins at the end of my term.

Leadership and Management Success Tip

Merely having followers is not always enough. Sometimes they require training to turn their willingness into ability.

THE PURSUIT OF PERFECTION

The Good and Bad of Hiring a Perfectionist

Do you want a staff of perfectionists? Some managers say "yes," whereas others respond with a resounding "no." The informed answer is, "it all depends." Here's why:

Of that portion of the population who are perfectionists, some are blindly or proudly so. Others are aware of possessing this characteristic and informed about it. I call them recovering perfectionists. I know because I am one.

A self-aware perfectionist understands this condition, knowing how to tap into and celebrate the many strengths and benefits of pursuing excellence. At the same time, they know to guard against its limiting, self-defeating, and even paralyzing facets.

Doing research on perfectionism reveals a host of debilitating traits, starting with compulsiveness and going downhill from there. Self-aware perfectionists, however, can tap into the positive aspects of their natural tendencies when appropriate. At the same time, they can seek to avoid having perfectionism's alluring snares handicap them.

The Upside of Perfectionism

For a perfectionist, there are many traits which provide immense value in the workplace. Here are four considerations:

Produce Quality Work: Perfectionists take pleasure in excellence and find satisfaction in a job done well. They produce high-quality work. *Good enough* is not in their vocabulary. They often do more than expected, sometimes more than needed. But their outcomes are awe inspiring.

Exceed Expectations: If the boss requests a summary, the perfectionist will submit a report. If achieving a 99 percent rating is admirable, the purist will aim for 99.9—and then 100. Being above average is unacceptable. Being the best is a self-imposed requirement. Anything less is failure.

Go the Extra Mile: Perfectionists often give more than asked. If a report needs to be five pages long, they'll turn in six—maybe ten. If a product needs to have three new features, they will add a fourth and then a fifth. If they set a record last month, they'll strive to better it this month.

An example from sports is shooting free throws while the rest of the team showers. Another is doing an extra thirty minutes of batting practice—every day.

Set High Standards: Another trait is that perfectionists set exacting standards, both for themselves and others. If the standards are attainable, it's acceptable, and even admirable, for the perfectionist to set a bar high for him or herself.

The Downside of Perfectionism

Of course, there are counterparts to these positive traits. Here are three:

Procrastination: One is procrastination. Often the perfectionist subconsciously reasons that the result of their work will never be exactly right—no matter how much time they invest—so why start?

In fact, they delay the project until the last possible moment, so there is a plausible excuse as to why it's not perfect: "I didn't have much time to work on it!"

Delayed Decision-Making: Another side effect associated with perfectionism is having problems making quick decisions. Sometimes they need to "sleep on it" to gauge the correctness of their judgment. Other times, decisions can be agonizingly difficult for them to reach. Taking this to an extreme, some perfectionists miss deadlines and blow past due dates, often agonizing over some trivial detail.

They fear coming to the wrong conclusion—that is, a less than perfect one. They delay a decision while awaiting more information, so they can conduct an informed analysis. Unfortunately, amassing more data seldom cures their mental paralysis.

Never Done: When the perfectionist completes their work by the specified date, they'll often second-guess themselves and insist on making changes after the fact. Not only does this unnecessarily delay the next steps, without wise management they may never deem a project as truly done.

High Expectations: As mentioned above, perfectionists set lofty standards for themselves. And they often foist their faultlessness on others. This does little more than establish the groundwork for future frustration, disappointment, and conflict between the precision-minded and the rest of the world.

Hiring Perfectionists

Over the years I have interviewed many perfectionists. As it becomes apparent that I'm talking to one, I segue into a special line of questioning, just for them.

"So," I inquire, "do you consider yourself to be a perfectionist?"

Their responses fall into one of three categories.

Denial: The first one is shock. If a person who has just exhibited several perfectionist traits acts appalled or denies any connection, I judge them to either be disingenuous or lacking in self-awareness. Neither are characteristics I want in an employee.

Pride: The second type of response to my perfectionist query is unabashed pride and smug satisfaction in possessing this quality. To make sure I'm not rushing to a snap judgment, I give them one last chance for redemption. "What," I ask, "do you see as the weaknesses of being a perfectionist?"

Occasionally, they'll comprehend the importance of that question, using an astute answer to move them from this category over to category three. Usually, however, they give me a blank stare, as if my question was nonsensical, responding that there is no downside or that they don't understand what I asked.

In a similar fashion, I don't want to work with a perfectionist who fails to realize the turmoil they can produce by their proclivity for perfection.

Self-Aware: The third type of perfectionist applicant smiles at this question. They share their self-awareness about the shortcomings of how perfectionism manifests itself in them. With insight, they identify the less-than-admirable ways that it reveals itself in them and share how they'll guard themselves from this tendency.

This is a person I want on my team.

Yes, they may require a bit more management effort at times, but doing so is worth the extra energy because the result will be an employee who produces quality work, frequently exceeds expectations, does more than expected, and sets ambitious standards for him or herself.

Isn't this who you want working in your organization too?

Leadership and Management Success Tip

Master the art of interviewing perfectionists and learn how to manage them.

A STRATEGIC BLUNDER

Broken Promises Result in Disillusionment

I was once on the board of a local nonprofit service organization. When my stint ended, I didn't qualify for a second term, but there were two roles I could move into. One was a task I disliked. The other was a challenge I relish—strategic planning.

I told the executive director I was interested in leading the strategic planning initiative but was concerned about forming a committee. My interest gleefully excited him, and he assured me he would put together the committee for me. All I had to do was lead the team and guide the plan development.

I waited, and I waited. After weeks of silence, I asked the executive director how he was doing at finding committee members.

"I was thinking about that," he said. "You don't need a committee. You can handle it just as well by yourself."

I knew in my gut he was wrong. I knew that better results occur from a group decision-making process. Yet I also knew that navigating group dynamics would take much longer. Bubbling with overconfidence, I believed I could produce a great strategic plan by myself. I accepted his assessment.

I went to work right away, thrilled with the challenge before me. Few things would have excited me more. I kept him apprised of my progress, sending monthly email updates.

Several months later I presented him with my finished strategic plan. It was innovative and would move the organization forward in fresh ways.

Though his response to my plan was tactful, I doubted he liked it. In retrospect, I suspect he wanted a plan that would merely affirm what he was already doing. But that's not what I gave him. I had presented him with something unconventional, something groundbreaking.

Assuming I was on the right track, I waited for

the opportunity to present my strategic plan to the board. That opportunity never came.

Without my knowledge, the executive director forwarded my strategic plan to an academic outside our organization. The man soundly dismissed my ideas with disdain. He did this largely because I had the audacity to form my recommendations without group input. Never mind that doing this solo was exactly what the executive director had told me to do.

I persisted in trying to get traction with my strategic plan, but nothing happened. Though the executive director gave me a brief time during each board meeting to talk about aspects of my vision, he controlled the scope of what I could cover and limited discussion. My year-long stint as their strategic planner ended quietly, with no acknowledgment.

Over the years, I had heard whispered implications that the director was at times underhanded and not to trust him. I dismissed those as rumors, but now I had experienced them firsthand and knew them to be correct.

Though I was behind what this organization stood for and did, I'd lost respect for the director and therefore interest in the organization's mission.

The director's inconsistent instructions to me

and poor leadership turned a once-passionate supporter into a disillusioned dissenter.

Leadership and Management Success Tip

Every person we interact with can choose to support our cause or oppose it. Therefore, it's critical to treat every person with respect and not do anything to abuse or misuse your relationship with them.

RECOGNIZE AND REACT TO OPPORTUNITIES

The Unexpected Can Be a Gift and We Shouldn't
Squander It

My employer once tasked me with turning around an unprofitable subsidiary of the company. Two people preceded me in this effort and failed. I suspect, however, that they were unprepared to deal with the momentous task in front of them. Overwhelmed, they didn't know what to do. I did. And I embraced the challenge.

I began my work offsite and interacted with the office manager by phone. I determined three things to address and set about making them happen.

First, I needed to hold the manager accountable for her mismanagement and guide her to change her methods. Second, I had to find expenses to cut. Third, I wanted to optimize operations for increased efficiency.

Though it was all straightforward and doable, it would also take time. I developed a strategy of what to do, the order to do it, and when to complete it. My plan was sound.

When I arrived on site for my first visit, I added a fourth item to my list: energize a disenfranchised workforce. They didn't believe anyone cared about them. And based on how their manager treated them, they were right. I needed to change that.

Yes, I still did my planned work on the first three items on my list, but I made sure I spent as much time with the staff as possible. I came in early and stayed late so I would be around for their scheduled shifts. As I worked in their proximity, I observed, I listened, and we talked.

Many had legitimate complaints about working conditions, and some offered astute suggestions for improvement. One employee pointed out an inefficient configuration in their office.

I agreed with her. "Let's fix it."

Wide-eyed and mouth agape, she watched me

implement her suggestion. It took me about ten minutes.

"No one's ever done anything like this for us before." Her eyes misted over.

For the rest of my time there, I spent every extra moment I could working to address the employees' concerns. I fixed things. I threw away junk. And I streamlined processes. As I did, their appreciation for me grew and their attitude toward their work changed.

Though my supervisor later questioned the priority I placed on doing things he deemed as inconsequential and not solely focused on my three objectives, I assured him it was exactly what those employees needed.

Over the following months, I made more trips there and implemented additional improvements. The staff began to anticipate my arrival and appreciated our interaction. Their attitudes improved, and they stopped complaining. Instead, they offered suggestions.

The accounting department tracked my progress and gave me monthly financial reports. What started out as a significant shortfall soon changed to a small one, and then to break even. After six months, we made a profit, albeit a small one. It was the ideal time to sell the subsidiary, and we did.

Leadership and Management Success Tip

What appears to be the most pressing issue isn't always what matters the most or produces the best results.

CRISIS MANAGEMENT

React with Courage to the Unexpected

My employer had just undergone a rightsizing effort to optimize our workforce and strengthen our financial situation. A result of this was that I now had two departments to manage instead of one. I also had twice the staff. I embraced this challenge with enthusiasm, implementing changes to merge the two departments into one cohesive unit.

On Friday, as I wrapped up the workweek, my boss poked his head into my office and asked if I'd be in town on Saturday.

Unsure of his peculiar question, I nodded.

"I may call you to come into the office for a meeting. Make sure you're available." Without further explanation, he left.

I wasn't sure if I should be worried or excited. On Saturday morning, my phone rang. It was my boss. His tone, more blunt than usual, filled me with apprehension. He summoned me to the office.

Upon arrival, he informed me that our effort at rightsizing fell far short. To stay in business, we needed to slash expenses by the end of the month. The only way to do that was to prune the workforce.

In quick order, he told me three key pieces of information. First, he gave me the names of five members of my staff I would have to lay off on Monday morning. Next, he gave me three more departments to manage. Third, he told me which of the staff from my new departments would remain. He would lay off the rest.

My assignment was to develop a plan by Monday morning to make everything function and maintain all essential work.

Though sad for my coworkers who would lose their jobs, I dove into the challenge of developing a plan to make everything mesh. By Monday morning I was ready.

Laying off five employees—for no fault of their

own—was draining. Yet once that was behind me, I excitedly implemented my planned changes, in a strategically determined order, to bring about the needed structure to move forward.

Although I let go of many secondary efforts, I established a structure to effectively deal with all essential aspects of my five departments without negatively impacting customers.

We were in crisis mode, and I thrived under the challenge.

Though I excel at responding well to major problems as they come up, I've often struggled to recognize incremental changes that occur gradually.

What I didn't see was our company slowly moving out of crisis mode and returning to a more stable situation. But I stayed in crisis mode and didn't move out of it. It took my boss reassigning me to a different position for me to see my error.

I do, however, credit him for developing a plan to keep the company afloat. And I'm proud of the role I played to help make that happen. I only wish I'd been better able to navigate the aftermath.

At the beginning of this book, I mentioned times of my leadership success and times of leadership failure. In retrospect, I see that most of the times I deem as *failures* resulted from me not seeing and reacting to the minor shifts that occurred on a day-to-day basis.

Guard against repeating my mistake.

Leadership and Management Success Tip

It's critical to recognize and react to the monumental changes that inevitably occur in business, as well as the incremental shifts that pop up in every organization and in any job.

LEAD BY EXAMPLE

Be Fair with Your Staff

I once led a service department that provided telephone customer support for specialized, high-tech equipment and software. We staffed our office during regular business hours, Monday through Friday. And we rotated handling on-call to cover emergency situations that arose in the evenings, on weekends, and on holidays.

I sought to evenly distribute on-call responsibilities throughout the staff. I also took my fair share, something that not all my predecessors had done.

During my time managing this department, I strove to add professionalism and increase quality service to what initially started as an informal and unstructured effort. One item I implemented was a Monday morning staff meeting. This was to update everyone about what had occurred over the weekend, communicate ongoing issues needing attention, and set goals for the week.

The meetings started at 8 a.m., even though some employees viewed this starting time as more of a suggestion. As a result, I struggled to have everyone present for the entire Monday morning staff meetings. Though I dared not fire anyone for their tardiness, I had an effective option to motivate a change in their behavior: on-call assignments.

One Monday morning, the lack of priority my staff had given to arriving on time for the meeting especially frustrated me. I proclaimed that next Monday, anyone who was late would be on call for the entire week. At last, I got their attention.

That weekend my family and I went out of town for a much-needed break. We returned late Sunday night to six inches of slushy snow in our driveway. Exhausted from the long drive, I didn't try to clear the snow and pulled the car into the garage. I would deal with the snow Monday night.

I arose the next morning dismayed to find that the once-slushy snow had turned into an impassable path of frozen slush and ice shards. It took me forty minutes of frustration, heaping abuse on my poor car, to cross the fifty-foot-long driveway and reach the neatly plowed road.

I reached work to find everyone present, smirking at my late arrival. I swallowed hard, told them I would handle on call for the next seven days, and launched into our meeting.

From then on, no one was ever late for our staff meetings.

Leadership and Management Success Tip

Hold yourself to the same standard—and even a higher one—that you hold your staff to.

CUSTOMER SERVICE FAILURE

Consider the Complete Picture to Ensure Success

Getting my annual income tax return done is one of my most dreaded tasks. Though I keep excellent records and prepare throughout the year, tax time produces much anxiety. One year, as I organized the year's documents for my accountant, I stumbled upon two contradictory statements from the same company.

Until I knew which one to trust, I couldn't move forward.

Fearing the ordeal before me, I noticed the forms gave a toll-free number, with an extension. This was a most customer-centric sign. I envisioned a quick resolution with a rational explanation for the conflicting numbers. With expectation, I dialed the number and punched in the extension.

A man answered my call quickly. He was cheerful. This was a good sign. I explained my dilemma as concisely as possible and held my breath.

"Oh, you're an existing customer." He sighed. I had reached a sales line, and he didn't want to talk to me.

"What's your account number?" His disdain oozed.

I gave him the number from the statement.

"That's not one of *our* account numbers." His irritation came through the phone. He groaned. "What's your soc?"

His use of an abbreviation heightened my irritation. He was in a hurry, and I was in his way. It's sloppy to use slang or internal abbreviations when talking with customers. I gave him my social security number. Then *I* sighed.

"Can't find that either. You sure you're calling the right place?"

I reminded him I had called the number on the form that *his* company had sent me.

"Must be your account's been closed."

I assured him it wasn't. He murmured some more, then placed me on hold.

After waiting too long, a woman picked up the line. He had done a blind transfer of my call. With similar abruptness, but a slightly gentler disposition, she asked for the same information. "Let me check something," she said at last.

She placed me on hold. I endured another long wait and another blind transfer.

This time, however, the lady who answered was as skilled at customer service as the others were not. Within a few seconds, I regained my hope for a positive outcome. Despite a five-minute interlude and two unacceptable agents, my initial optimism reemerged.

She apologized when I shared the failure of her coworkers. I assured her it wasn't her fault. By this time, she had retrieved my records and given a thorough explanation of the information on both forms.

"Our department is our company's best-kept secret," she said with a polite laugh. "They don't even know we exist."

My ordeal exposed three points of failure with this company. The first was a less-than-ideal phone number or extension listed on their statement—or the failure to route that number or extension properly. The second was people answering the phone who lacked customer service skills or training. And the third was a department that not all employees knew about.

This resulted in wasted time and frustration for both me and the first two employees.

Leadership and Management Success Tip

Pursue a comprehensive approach to customer-facing interaction, with an eye toward customer service excellence and operational effectiveness.

A CASE STUDY IN HOW NOT TO
TREAT EMPLOYEES

Your Management Style Produces Either Success or
Failure

After spending the prior summer relegated to working a smattering of part-time odd jobs, my son, Dan, desired a different outcome for his summer break from college. He learned the importance of starting his search early to beat the competition.

Through networking, he developed a list of prime prospects. Four opportunities emerged, each with an inside contact to guide the process, offer advice, and provide feedback. Dan's summer employment prospects seemed bright.

During spring break, he met with each company, submitting resumes, completing applications, and going through interviews. Each opportunity looked promising. Soon he was analyzing their respective merits and desirability as his ideal summer job, ranking them in order of preference. With all these encouraging opportunities, it was hard for him to pursue new leads or less desirable options.

Dan maintained contact with the companies throughout the rest of the school year and made plans to meet as soon as school was out. During those follow-up meetings, things unraveled.

Because of unforeseen events, two employers backed away from their summer hiring plans during that first week. Two weeks later, a third bowed out and eventually the fourth fell through. Now Dan was a month out of school and had to restart his job search. Fortunately, the area high schools were still in session, so at least he could get a jump on their impending onslaught on the job market.

Amid desperation, he did an internet job search. The job site allowed him to conduct his search for businesses within a specified radius of home. He put in five miles and—although in a rural area—he got a match.

What follows is a sad saga of how not to recruit, manage, or treat staff. Within it are lessons on how to churn employees.

Hide Key Information

The help wanted ad lacked tangible details. It didn't specify the type of work, providing only vague generalities. The verbiage was something like "exciting and rewarding position, working with other professionals at an established and successful company."

It was hard not to get excited and draw the conclusion that he had stumbled onto the most wonderful career opportunity available. As it turned out, this was not the case.

Misrepresent the Facts

Dan responded to the ad and had a phone interview. An in-person meeting was the next step. It was in another city, over thirty miles away. Given the high price of gas and his limited funds, this was a discouraging development for a job represented to be within five miles of home.

Believing that only this initial meeting would be at a distant location, he proceeded. After three hours of a preliminary group interview and a subsequent one-on-one conversation, he received a job offer from BJ, his new boss. He would sell knives. Then he received more disconcerting news. Three days of training would also occur at that distant location.

Mandated twice-a-week sales meetings would begin after training. Not surprisingly, they were also in that faraway city. BJ also required Dan to make twice-a-day long-distance phone calls to check in. It was adding up to be quite expensive for this *local* job. On top of that, he had to buy his demo knives at a cost of over $100.

Hold Purposeless Meetings

Not deterred, Dan proceeded. He made a sale as soon as his training ended and headed off to his first sales meeting. So as not to interfere with selling, BJ scheduled the sales meetings at nine in the evening, which was too late to make appointments. The meeting wasn't what Dan expected. BJ lacked a plan for the meeting and meandered through it. There was no apparent intent—other than possibly to see who would show up.

The meetings would start late and had little substance. Other times BJ would not be able to locate his materials. More than once Dan and his cohorts waited while BJ made copies, talked on the phone, or left the room. Once he got mad at the people not present and chewed out those who were.

Waste Time

During these meetings, BJ put off questions for afterward. If Dan waited around to have his questions answered, he might not get home until after midnight. Often, the responses to his questions frustrated him, receiving cocky retorts or more delays.

The twice-a-day phone calls were also frustrating. Dan would alter his schedule to make these calls at the prescribed time. Although BJ required these calls, sometimes he wasn't available, or he might respond with irritation at the interruption. During these calls, sometimes he encouraged Dan. But most of the time, BJ chastised Dan for not doing more and would dismiss his questions.

Undervalue Staff

Another problem was BJ's focus on hiring more

sales staff. He gave priority to recruitment and had little left to give his existing charges. From Dan's original group, the attrition rate was at 90 percent after two weeks. BJ viewed staffing as a numbers game. It was quantity over quality. People were expendable, and he needed to hire many for a few to stick.

Make Unreasonable Demands

The twice-a-week sales meetings and twice-a-day phone calls struck Dan as unreasonable, especially since he could see little reason for them and experienced no benefit. Most telling, however, was BJ's insistence that they work seven days a week—for a job advertised as part-time. More infuriating was BJ bragging that when he was in the field, he would only sell a few days a week.

Give Wrong Advice

When the sales staff would complain about the cost of driving to sales meetings and making long-distance calls, BJ would dismissively respond that it was all tax deductible. He claimed to be aggressive in filling out his tax forms and boasted that he generally paid no taxes. He implied his staff should follow his example.

Don't Pay What You Promise

BJ promised Dan a minimum guaranteed amount on every appointment, regardless of the results. Never once did this happen, with no reason revealed. It could be that there were many loopholes in the policy, allowing ample wiggle room to avoid paying the minimum reimbursement. Possibly BJ exercised discretion over this facet and abused his power. Or maybe it was merely a false promise.

Arbitrarily Refuse Training

Dan's initial training covered product knowledge and how to do a demonstration. One item was to ask for referrals after every presentation, regardless of if he made a sale. Dan accumulated leads but awaited training on how to follow through.

He asked BJ what to do. BJ's response was that he'd cover it at the sales meetings. Except he didn't.

Dan soon gave up on the sales meetings and

asked BJ directly for help. BJ's unexpected rejoinder was, "Since you're not coming to the meetings anymore, I'm not going to tell you."

Despite all this, Dan did well selling knives. He enjoyed making presentations and doing demos. This resulted in a high closing ratio, and he quickly earned a boost in his commission rate. Soon after Dan embarked on his knife-selling adventure, another job opportunity availed itself. It was mowing lawns and doing landscaping. The work was part-time and only expected to last for three weeks. Wanting to keep his options open, Dan balanced both jobs.

He soon realized that not all bosses were like BJ. His landscaping boss was easygoing and flexible. He and Dan quickly established a rapport and worked well together. Although the job was never more than part-time, it continued for the rest of the summer.

Dan continued as a knife salesman, though it became so part-time as to be negligible. The outcome would have been quite different if only he had received the additional training he asked for and been treated with a bit of respect.

[Epilogue: BJ later emailed Dan that the office would be "temporarily shut down" and the sales reps reassigned to other offices. BJ would go back to being a field rep.]

Leadership and Management Success Tip

Letting people move into management before they're ready hurts them, your brand, and your employees.

THE ONLY CONSTANT IS CHANGE

Transitioning from What Was to What Is Requires
Intentionality

A s I look back, I see how things have changed. I have changed, my family has changed, technologies have changed, my business has changed, and the industries I work in have changed.

In today's business environment, a culture of change is essential for every organization. In my younger days, I would recommend change for the sheer fun of it. Now, older and wiser, I only advocate change when there is a genuine reason to do so.

For most people, change is hard.

Change takes something familiar and replaces it with something unknown. Each organization has people who are change resistant. Each leader, manager, and supervisor knows exactly who these people are. With such folks, their aversion to change varies from unspoken trepidation to overt confrontation. Regardless of the manifestation, we need to be compassionate, realizing that these reactions are merely their way of responding to fear—fear of the unknown.

To establish a change-oriented culture in our organizations, the first step is to minimize employee fears toward change. As covered in the chapter, "How to Best Deal with Change," most of the time, employees can accept change if:

1. the change is incremental and small,
2. they have some input or control over the change, and
3. they understand the reason for the change.

The key is communication. Address change head-on. For every change, employees wonder how it will affect them.

Could they lose their job?

Might they face a cut in their hours?

Will they have to work harder than they already are?

Will they need to do something unpleasant?

What happens if they can't learn the new skills?

These are all worries, worries about the unknown. As with most worries, the majority will never happen. But with a lack of reliable information and top-down assurances, these irrational worries take on a life all their own.

Successfully orchestrating change requires effective communication. Not just once, but ongoing. Not only to key staff, but to all employees. And not by one method, but by several: group meetings, written correspondence, and one-on-one discussions. A true and effective open-door policy helps too. It's also critical to set a positive attitude at the beginning, from the top of the organization, which never wavers. Celebrate milestones, generously thank staff along the way, and provide reasonable rewards at the end.

Successfully taking these steps will send a powerful signal to staff. Even though the change may still concern them, they will find comfort knowing they have accurate information. And for each successful change, the next one becomes easier to bring about.

We'll know we have successfully created a change-friendly organization when our employees —all of them—get bored with the status quo and seek change on their own. They will ask for more challenging work, desire to expand their job, and want to add innovative technology.

At this point, the potential of our organizations becomes unlimited; the personal growth of our staff, unshackled; and the future, inviting. We don't know what that future will entail, only that things will change for the better.

So, sit back and enjoy the ride, fully confident that the only constant is change.

Leadership and Management Success Tip
Learn to manage change, or it will manage you.

FINDING A GOOD MANAGER

Understand the Pros and Cons of Two Options

This simple statement occurs too often. "I need to find a good manager."

I've heard it many times over the years as a business consultant and experienced it firsthand as a business owner. Despite the straightforward nature of this basic need, a successful outcome is anything but easy. If you make the wrong selection, the future is in jeopardy, be it for the department, the office, or the entire operation. It only takes a few months of mismanagement to undo years of work spent building a smooth-functioning machine.

The problem is that leaders seldom see this downward spiral until after the damage occurs. By then, exemplary employees have left, remaining staff is demoralized, and longtime customers leave. Cyberspace is abuzz.

Despite the careful vetting process, employment screens, interviews, background checks, and personal references, your handpicked manager—the superstar who would solve all your problems and make your job easier—has failed to meet expectations.

Once again, you're pressed to find a manager. The options before you are deceptively simple. There are only two: promote from within or hire from without.

Promote from Within

When you promote existing employees into management, there are several benefits. First, you know them and their work ethic. Next, they've already proven themselves, perhaps as a supervisor, a trainer, a star employee, or maybe all three. Third, they know your business. They won't need training in how your organization operates. Last, they know the industry and they understand your company.

The downside is they seldom have management experience. This requires management training, followed by close supervision as they grow in their job. This will not happen quickly. Along the way, they will make mistakes. We hope their blunders will be minor and the successes will surpass their errors.

My preference is to promote managers from within. I do this whenever possible, as I prefer to develop employees for job growth and groom them for advancement. The problem is that supply seldom matches demand. That is, when I need to promote someone into management, the candidates may not be ready. Or the employees are ready to take on more, but there are no openings, and they leave.

Then my only option is to hire from the outside.

Hire from Without

The other approach is to hire an experienced manager. This solves all the issues surrounding management training. Yes, the new manager will still require some oversight at first, but the time will be much shorter than for someone with no managerial experience.

The disadvantage of hiring from the outside is

that you have no history together. You don't know their work ethic or character, and they don't know your business or operation. They lack specific relevant experience and don't understand your industry. And if they have industry expertise, you may need to retrain them to fit your organization.

Personally, I have experienced little success when hiring managers from outside the company. In fact, I don't recall a single time when this worked for the long term. All my longstanding managers have come from within, though I admit this may be a result of my personality and management style. Therefore, don't take my experience as a given. Your results may differ.

Conclusion

There's no simple approach when hiring a manager, with no right answer or ideal solution. It's part timing and part chance, but you can tip the balance in your favor. This challenge makes running a business or nonprofit fun. After all, if anyone could do it, everyone would.

Leadership and Management Success Tip

Understanding the pitfalls of finding a good manager is your first step to realizing a successful outcome.

KICK THE CAN DOWN THE ROAD

Don't Leave for Someone Else What You Can Do Today

An association ran a nonprofit service bureau to handle their members' telephone communications 24/7.

They hired me to come in for a consulting assignment. The managing director initially contacted me. But it was at her boss's prompting. She asked me to spend a week there to assess the service and recommend improvements.

Her superior, the association's president that year, however, had a different agenda. He believed she was the organization's weak link. His expectation was that I would confirm it. Assuming that was the case, he wanted me to draft a report to that effect for the board and recommend how to best move forward.

Time was a critical element. The board's presidency changed every year, moving from one doctor to the next. And the current president had already begun his term.

For several years, each board president had been unwilling to address the management issue at their service or had been unable to see it. Instead, they had put in their time as board president and hoped their successor would take care of the problem. In essence, they kicked the can down the road.

The current president wanted to resolve the problem and not pass it on to his replacement. By bringing in a highly paid industry consultant, he expected my report to motivate the board to approve him to act.

When I arrived at the service bureau, it was quite apparent that his assessment was correct. The managing director had a hands-off style and made no effort to lead her staff. She would arrive late, take long lunches, and leave early. She seemed to spend more time pursuing personal interests than working on the organization's needs.

I met individually with each member of the staff.

With no prodding on my part, a common threat emerged. No one respected her and few people liked her. Her underpaid assistant handled the day-to-day work, putting in many hours to complete it all.

I estimated that the managing director spent four hours a day doing her job. Her counterparts at other companies put in ten to twelve hours a day to do the job correctly.

Having confirmed that the managing director was indeed the weak link, I set about the task of recommending her replacement. My preference is always to promote from within.

The assistant was the best candidate, as she was already doing most of the work. But she lacked skills and experience in other areas. Had there been someone to train and mentor her, I'm sure she would have done a wonderful job as managing director. But with no one to fill that role (I would leave in a few days), I worried that moving her into that position before she was ready would cause frustration on her part and disappointment for everyone else.

Instead, I recommended they consider hiring someone from outside the organization who had industry management experience. And I recommended a certain person who could do the job and was looking for a new opportunity.

I said goodbye to the staff and flew home to complete my report. It was exactly what the board president wanted, and the board gave him permission to act. He fired the existing managing director and hired the man I recommended.

Though I never had ongoing interactions with him or the organization, I did find out that the new managing director excelled in the position and met everyone's objectives.

The board president could have taken the simple path and left the managerial problem at the service bureau for his successor to deal with. Instead, he took the bold step to act and bring about the needed change.

I'm sure this took much more time than he planned to give the job as board president, and it detracted from his work, but he took the bold step to handle it. He didn't kick the can down the road for someone else to deal with later.

Leadership and Management Success Tip

Successful leadership means doing what needs to be done, when it needs to be done, regardless of if it's convenient or easy.

KICK THE CAN, PART 2

A Rare Case When Inaction Is Better than Action

Recall the parachurch organization where I was board president. I gave needed structure to the board meetings, trained the board members to be more effective, and groomed my successor. But this isn't where the story ends.

With a few months left in my term as president, the vice president resigned unexpectedly. Though I had shared my concern that he was spending too much time on the organization and not enough on his own business, he dismissed my worry. By the time he realized that his business desperately needed him—all of him—he had no time left to continue as vice president or assume the role of presidency.

At about this same time I realized a sobering truth. With my focus on the board, I had neglected a greater problem. Though a likable person and passionate about her work, the organization's executive director—the one who asked me to join the board—was ineffective at her position. She was holding the organization back. She needed to go.

As president, it was my responsibility to do this. But the timing was awful. We had no vice president and no suitable candidate to fill that role. My term would end in a few months, so the executive director was the only person who could provide any sort of continuity. Letting her go at this critical time would have resulted in a complete vacuum in the organization. It could implode.

Though I didn't like it, I reasoned that the best thing I could do in this circumstance was to do nothing. I concluded it was best to leave her in place and let someone else deal with the problem later. To my dismay, I kicked the can down the road.

A few months after my presidency ended, I received a phone call from a president who had served the board many years ago. I didn't know her, and she didn't know me. She explained that she was meeting with as many past presidents as possible to get insight to best lead the organization forward. Since I was the most recent president, she had great interest in what I had to say.

Though she was acting as president for a time, it wasn't a role she wanted to fill long term. But she was willing to do what she had to in order to keep the organization afloat.

We talked about the situation and the needs of the organization. I lamented that the scope of work for the executive director had outgrown her abilities. But it turned out my assessment was too generous. I had misunderstood the situation.

The executive director was hired for the position because she was a loyal volunteer. She had no experience in that role and was never effective at it. She needed to go. But the problem was finding a replacement.

The board lacked the budget to hire a qualified executive director for any more than a few hours a week, but the needs of the organization called for someone closer to full-time.

The former president's idea was to hire a qualified executive director with the understanding that he or she would need to raise funds to cover the difference between the current budget for the executive director and what they deserved to make.

The organization had a few supporters who could contribute much more than they were currently, but they were holding back until better management was in place. I challenged the former president to secure pledges for the new executive director's salary for the first year. This would allow him or her to work on the operations side of things first without a need to immediately begin fundraising. She liked the idea and ended up implementing a scaled-back version of it.

Soon the new executive director was in place. I had a bit of interaction with him as he took on his new role, but not much—because he didn't need it. I soon moved out of the area and lost contact with the organization, but I understand the new executive director was still there several years later. It seems both he and the organization were doing fine.

Leadership and Management Success Tip

Though sometimes the right course—the only option—is to do nothing, we should seek opportunities to help fix later what we couldn't fix today.

THE EFFECTS OF HIGH
UNEMPLOYMENT

Treat Your Staff Well to Keep from Needing to Find
New Employees

A t one time, the unemployment rate was running high. Businesses needing to hire found themselves in a *buyer's market*. This is worth noting because we may one day return to that scenario. Here is a snapshot from that era.

In times of high unemployment, there are plenty of people looking for work. This results in more applicants to consider for each opening. It limits employment options, reducing worker mobility. The result is that employee churn rates are—or at least should be—low. Having more applicants to pick from and less staff leaving by choice should indicate a stable workforce. Unfortunately, this may not be the case. And even if it is, it affords a false security.

Consider the following five employees:

Chuck worked in a small satellite office of a large organization. The staff there was close and functioned together well. They cared for each other and were like family. They helped each other complete their work and serve clients, regardless of job description and title.

Sadly, this idyllic reality ended when corporate closed Chuck's office to save money. They fired some staff but permitted Chuck to work remotely from home. Then Chuck got a new boss, who rescinded that offer. Chuck had to commute 120 miles each day to work.

The corporate office was nothing like his old one. Finger-pointing and passively following job descriptions replaced teamwork. No one cared about the clients or each other. One by one, Chuck's coworkers quit or were fired. He fears he'll be next and frantically looks for comparable work closer to home.

Carly is a college graduate whose chosen profession currently has a 40 percent unemployment rate. Unable to find work, she went to graduate school. Her summer employment is offering her a full-time position when she graduates but has been vague on the details. (She did computer work no one else wanted to do).

Unfortunately, this job isn't in her field of study, nor does it interest her. However, out of necessity, she may have to take this job. Even if she does, she doesn't expect to remain long.

Danielle also recently graduated from college. Her college internship continued after graduation, with the promise of a promotion when the economy turned around. Her work aligned with her education, but without the title, recognition, or pay.

This went on for a year. Although she worked full time, it was at her part-time hourly internship rate—or 40 percent of what's typical. She is polishing her resume and seeks better-paying alternatives.

Karl has a full-time job in his chosen profession. At first, he liked his company and earned stellar reviews. In his latest review—the first by his new manager—he scored the lowest in each category.

Last year, after their busy season ended, the company fired a hardworking colleague. Karl worries he might get the axe as soon as the seasonal peak ends. His salaried position carries the expectation of working an additional twenty-five hours a week during the busy season. His boss, however, recently tacked on an additional ten.

He desperately wants to find a new job but is working too much to have time to pursue it. As soon as things slow down, he'll begin his job hunt in earnest.

Larry enjoyed working in his chosen career, finding it rewarding and fulfilling. After a planned move out of state, however, he was unable to find work at his level of experience and education. He eventually took a much lower position at half the pay.

The company promotes from within, so he hoped he would eventually move into a position matching his skills and have his compensation restored. But because he functioned in a low-level position, the company continually overlooked him, despite him having more experience than some of his colleagues who received promotions.

The circumstances became so dreadful that he left, taking an even greater pay cut in exchange for a nicer place to work. Once again, he expects to earn a promotion. Although feedback on his performance is favorable, there are no openings. He might need to switch jobs again.

Management Warnings

These people share two common characteristics.

First, they dislike their employers or their jobs. Some have endured lies, others have received harsh treatment, two are underpaid, and all are unhappy.

The other factor is that each of them desperately wants a different job and is working to make it happen. Since they have stellar qualifications and employable skills, their job expectations are realistic. When the economy turns around, they are sure to find better work.

From this we can interpolate that:

- Some employees are unhappy, but they continue to endure unsatisfactory work situations—for now—because they have to.
- Many people are underemployed. They'll correct that as soon as companies hire again. They represent their company's better employees, and they'll be the first to go.
- Some people are working outside their areas of expertise. For many, this is not a choice but a short-term necessity. They'll leave the first chance they get.

- When an entry-level employee sticks around after graduation, it may not necessarily mean that they like the company. They may just have no other options.

What does this mean?

- When the economy improves, many employees will immediately seek to advance their work situations. Some reports reveal that one third of the workforce is waiting to change jobs.
- The most employable people—the best workers—will be the first to switch. Those who lack skills or drive will stay.
- There is pent-up worker frustration, which employers will face when employment options emerge.

What can employers do?

- Act as though unemployment is low and it's a "seller's market." Treating employees better now, when you don't have to, will keep them working for you later, when they don't have to.

- Recognize that downsizing, hiring freezes, and consolidations have stretched employees and nearly pushed them to the breaking point. Seek ways to relieve stress and reduce their pressure now.
- Talk to employees and really listen. Listen for slights you can amend, injustices you can correct, and oversights you can make right.

You can take steps now to keep the employees you have, or you can wait for economic recovery and take steps then to find and train their replacements.

As expected, all five employees found new jobs once the economy turned around. Three found success quickly. The other two required more time, but they did leave.

Leadership and Management Success Tip

Treat your employees well in all situations. Though not all will appreciate it, some will, and they'll reward you with their loyalty.

THE EFFECTS OF LOW UNEMPLOYMENT

Discover How to Become a Company of Choice

Unemployment rates go in cycles, oscillating over the years between seasons of high unemployment and times of low unemployment. The prior chapter addressed a worker surplus. Now we'll consider a worker shortage.

During times of low unemployment, it's a *workers' market*. With too many positions going unfilled, people have their choice of jobs. This allows them to shop for the best opportunity.

As it relates to entry-level positions, they seek work that expects little and offers much in terms of compensation, flexibility, and benefits. It's hard to build an effective staff around these parameters.

The local outlet of a national quick-service restaurant recently added an enticement to the help wanted sign posted in front of their building. They now pay their employees the next day. I suspect it's the only way they can entice employees to show up for their scheduled shifts. Though this surprised me, it wasn't unexpected.

Last year a lawn service company resorted to paying its employees daily as well. The owner lamented that when he paid them weekly, most wouldn't show up for work the next day because they had money in their pockets. They only returned to work when they ran out of cash. His every-day-is-a-payday approach got him through the season and allowed most of his customers to get their lawns mowed promptly—at least most of the time.

Yet when he prepared for this season, he found it even harder to attract employees. In response, he canceled all his lawn-mowing contracts and closed that aspect of his business. He's shifting his focus to other activities that require fewer employees and produce better results.

If your business relies heavily on entry-level

employees, your primary problem during times of low unemployment may be simply getting them to show up for work. Of course, once they show up, you need them to do the work you hired them to do. Then you must strive to maintain their employment. It's a challenge you must deal with—somehow.

Yet it's not much different when hiring experienced workers for other positions. Finding them is the first challenge. Those that you consider are not likely going to be prime candidates. The best workers already have jobs. Many of the skilled workers in the labor pool during times of low unemployment are the lesser-qualified candidates, lacking the desired skills, experience, and work history.

Once hired—despite having the basic skills you need and being more apt to produce an acceptable outcome for their labor—their loyalty isn't assured. When another opportunity comes along that offers more, they'll be quick to leave. And you'll need to start the hiring process all over again.

Three Key Characteristics

It's even more critical to provide employment opportunities to attract workers and optimize retention during times of low unemployment. Though starting pay and benefits are the place to begin, compensation alone is not enough to attract and keep qualified staff.

In looking at businesses that don't struggle as much to maintain a viable workforce during times of low unemployment, I see less-tangible characteristics emerge. Three things stand out: a pleasant environment, supportive management, and happy coworkers.

1. A Nice Environment: Whether it's restaurants, retail, office, or production, the work environment is key. When workers struggle to find a job, they'll accept a workplace that's dirty, dingy, and distasteful. Yet when they have their choice of companies, they'll first judge you by the appearance of your facility. If it's clean, well-lit, and inviting they'll be more apt to pick yours as the workplace of choice than to go somewhere else.

2. Supportive Management: Next is management and supervision. When staff in these roles are professional, organized, and calm, they draw workers to them. Whether employees admit it or not, they crave structure. They're attracted to organizational excellence, like a flickering flame draws a moth.

Who wants to work for a boss who's sloppy,

muddled, and frazzled? Yet many of today's business leaders give off this exact vibe. It's no wonder they have trouble hiring staff.

3. Happy Coworkers: Third is the existing staff. If a job candidate arrives for an interview—or their first day of work—and sees happy employees going about their jobs, they want to be part of it. In contrast, when they see apathetic workers dragging themselves around and doing as little as possible, it sends the signal that this is a workplace to avoid.

Summary

Struggling to find and keep staff during times of low unemployment doesn't have to be the norm. With intentional effort, your business can be the exception.

Leadership and Management Success Tip

Make your operation be the workplace of choice. Then you won't have to accept substandard staffing during times of low unemployment.

SO, YOU'RE BEING ACQUIRED

Strive to Treat Your New Employees with Respect

Most employees fear the changes wrought by acquisition.

I have never been *acquired*, but I have been on the other side—about a dozen times—buying small and medium-sized companies and integrating them into a larger operation.

The almost universal response to an acquisition is panic. Employees, especially frontline staff, expect the worst. Even those who dislike their present company or the owner will protest loudly at the prospect of a new employer. Promises of increased pay, expanded benefits, and job security do little to quell their swelling apprehension. Theirs is a fear of the unknown.

Employees who work for a company that's acquired face some predictable scenarios.

One is that the buyer could want a working, functional facility, but not the staff. Conversely, the focus could be on the customer base, but not the staff or facility. In these cases, the facts are soon apparent, and the employees know their future employment status isn't good, but at least they know what to expect.

In most cases, however, the purchaser wants the entire operation: the staff, the facility, and the customers. Happily, jobs are secure, and the future is promising. Yes, changes will occur, but astute employees will anticipate and welcome these as expected adjustments for a better future. It is those who oppose or reject the new owner's directives who run the legitimate risk of unemployment.

When a subsidiary or division of a parent company is acquired, the possible outcomes are more complex. The intent could be to let the new acquisition continue to operate as is, in a hands-off, independent manner.

Some of the other prospects, however, aren't so encouraging. There could be a desire to cut costs, which means eliminating some positions or even departments. Sometimes, the goal is to sell off parts of the company to other buyers. The most extreme situation sees the entire company dismantled and sold piecemeal. Then those remaining employees will endure a second acquisition.

For those who acquire companies, never forget the human element. You are dealing with people's lives. Honestly communicate as much as you can, as quickly as you can. Back up your positive pronouncements with tangible supporting action. And if the news is bad, treat people with dignity, doing all you can to facilitate their movement into a new job.

For those being acquired, remember that, though you can't control much of what happens to you, you can control your response to it. Be realistic and update your resume so it's ready if needed, but don't prematurely jump ship. Instead, choose to have a positive attitude about the situation, support the new management, and prove yourself to be a valuable asset. You could end up pleasantly surprised by the result.

Leadership and Management Success Tip

When acquiring a company, view it from the employees' perspective to optimize successful outcomes with integrity.

THE SECRET TO SUCCESSFUL JOINT VENTURES AND STRATEGIC PARTNERSHIPS

Pitfalls to Avoid and Recommendations to Pursue

Astute entrepreneurs are always seeking ways to improve their business, increase revenue, and diversify into related business lines. During times of doubtful economic conditions, with possible decreased sales and smaller profits, it's even more critical to explore ways to bolster business.

One such way is by working with another organization for your mutual benefit. This concept goes by different labels, such as a joint venture, business alliance, strategic partnership, or collaboration. Often these arrangements are informal. At other times there is a more formal configuration, sometimes even resulting in a new legal entity established for this express purpose. Regardless of the name or resulting form, the effective consequence is that you now have a partner.

The results of these business alliances can be a sustained revenue stream, a short-term bump in income, or a wasted effort that leads to disappointment. In my experience, this latter outcome is common, but it doesn't need to be that way.

Careful planning now can help avert future disappointment and facilitate successful results for both parties. Before I share my recommendations, however, let's first explore why things often go awry:

Reasons for Failure

Looking for a Quick Fix: Most collaborations take time to produce results. The belief that you can reach an agreement one day and see results the next is unrealistic. It's prone to disillusionment.

If you pursue a joint venture as a last-ditch effort to save your business, it is too late. It's better to seek these types of innovative strategies while you are in a stable position and have the time to nurture and grow them. The payoff will not be quick, but when done right, it can be sustainable.

Not Willing to Contribute: Too often people enter partnership arrangements with the erroneous expectation that with little or no effort they'll realize great benefits from the partner company. This is selfish and shortsighted. Even if results initially occur, they won't last, as the partner has no reason to persist in doing all the work while you reap the benefits.

Pursuing a Win/Lose Agenda: Sometimes one or both parties in a business alliance holds a win/lose mentality. They persist in the belief that the only way for them to come out ahead is for their partner to lose.

Again, even if this works for a while, it won't last. In the end, it will produce accusation and heartache.

Taking Advantage of Your Partner: Other times joint venture partners carry a hidden agenda. Consider if there's some technology, information, or expertise that one party needs to share for the project to succeed. The partnership is merely a ruse to access that desired asset.

No one likes to be taken advantage of. When it occurs, ill will is inevitable and lawsuits are likely.

Inequitable Responsibilities and Rewards: Arrangements in which one party expends a greater amount of time and resources while realizing lesser results will fail. Business alliances where one party mostly gives, and the other party mostly takes, face failure from the start.

Lack of Agreed-upon Objectives and Measurements: If you don't know your target, how will you know if you reach it? How will you determine if the collaboration is working?

Stating that your aim is to increase sales is vague and untenable. Remember that a goal must be specific. It also needs to be quantifiable. Sometimes this is easy. Sometimes it isn't.

Let's say the goal is to increase staff morale. How do you measure that? One way might be to track the staff turnover rate, with a decrease in turnover implying an increase in morale. But is this sufficient and all-inclusive? Does your business partner concur? If your partner wants to measure morale by the number of employee complaints to management, with you focusing on the turnover stat, it's unlikely you'll agree on what success looks like.

No Exit Plan: It's unwise to assume a business alliance will last forever. Things change, and what may have been mutually beneficial will one day cease to be. Lacking a clear ending subjects participants to needless worry and anxiety.

Suppose one company needs to buy equipment, purchase inventory, or hire staff for the alliance to continue to function. If there is concern over how much longer the venture will last, there will certainly be reluctance to make the investments to continue it.

This results in tentative decision-making and could doom an otherwise healthy arrangement.

Recommendations for Success

With these pitfalls in mind, let's consider the

advice of how to embark upon a successful collaboration:

Be Forthright about Your Expectations and Contributions: This is not a time to hold back. Be clear about what you expect and what you'll do. Insist on the same attitude from the other person. Withholding key information will not give you a stronger position later but rather will make success less likely.

Pursue a Mutually Beneficial Relationship: If you can't find a win-win situation, there is really no point in persisting with discussions. Mutual benefit and satisfaction must occur to realize and sustain the outcomes.

Set Goals: Once you determine there is mutual benefit in moving forward, establish goals and expectations. As previously mentioned, these considerations must be agreed to and measurable.

Do Your Part: Whatever you agreed to do, be sure you follow up on it—or ensure that someone else does. Often those who agree to a joint venture aren't those tasked with implementing it.

Therefore, if you delegate responsibilities you agreed to handle, make sure they're clearly communicated and diligently pursued. If your team doesn't buy into the project or lacks commitment, the partnership will fail without producing the desired outcomes.

Discuss How and When the Arrangement Will End: Assume from the very start that the venture will someday end. Discuss what that point is and how to determine it, which shouldn't be hard if you were successful with the goal-setting recommendation.

Agree on the responsibilities of each company in dealing with resultant assets or remaining inventories in which one party may have a heavy investment. Determine how things can wind down in a controlled, ethical, and responsible manner so that minimal damage occurs to any stakeholders.

Summary

While there is much that can go awry in pursuing a business alliance, there is an exciting upside when implemented wisely. Aside from producing profitably sustainable results, some joint ventures have been more successful than either partner company, while others have become their own self-sustaining entity.

By avoiding the preceding pitfalls and pursuing the above recommendations, you'll set up your strategic partnership for success.

Leadership and Management Success Tip

Working with another organization for your mutual benefit will produce desired outcomes—if you proceed wisely.

CHOOSE BUSINESS ASSOCIATES
WITH CARE

Good or Bad, the Work of Those We Align with Reflects
on Us

Conference planners sometimes ask me to sit on a panel. The usual format is that each panelist makes an initial presentation, followed by a Q&A. Other times the presentations are longer, with no time for questions.

Most of my panel experiences have not been positive. For my first one, the other panel members dismissed my suggestion to coordinate our presentations. I went last. The first panelist covered some of my planned remarks, while the third person addressed all the rest. I had only a few minutes to develop fresh content.

Another time, at an early morning panel, one of the panelists had stayed up all night partying. Sitting next to me, he smelled like a brewery. With slurred speech and impaired judgment, his attempts at humor—some directed at me—were not funny. I spent the entire time praying he wouldn't get sick on me. I doubt he realized he made a fool of himself and demeaned the rest of us.

Another time I thought I was safe. Three of us discussed our remarks in advance, while the fourth person was vague, implying he would ad-lib something aligned with our presentations. He went just before me. The first two people gave practical advice, as was my plan, but the third guy delved into high-level theory, giving a well-conceived strategic vision for the future. He outclassed us all—and I had to follow him.

Not surprisingly, I no longer agree to sit on panels. I'm fine with solo presentations, where success or failure rests solely on me. But keep me away from group presentations.

In business, we often have occasions to collaborate with other companies. Like my panel opportunities, these seem easy to do, require less prep, and share risk. The key word is *seem*.

Here are three areas to consider:

Affiliate Marketing

Affiliate marketing is performance-based promotion, where one entity (a person or an organization) pays another entity for each lead or sale generated from the first entity. Often done via email, there is little cost and a potentially high payoff. Direct mail is another tactic. At a basic level, a company allows an ad aggregator to place relevant promotions on its website. The payoff is pay-per-click revenue.

I once bought a tutorial from someone I met at a convention. This person added me to his mailing list and began blasting out affiliate marketing pitches on a weekly basis, with multiple messages for each promotion. I grew weary of the hype and eventually unsubscribed, even though I was open to buying future products from him. Because of his implied endorsement of the people he promoted—some of whom I deemed questionable—and his unrelenting marketing for them, he lost me as a customer.

Strategic Alliances

Sometimes we seek opportunities to better serve clients by working with other businesses to provide a one-stop solution. Reselling products is one example, as is bundling services provided by other businesses.

When seamlessly integrated, customers don't realize they're dealing with two companies, and interaction occurs flawlessly. But when there's a problem, the customer sees only the initial company, blaming them for the shortcomings of its partner.

I once experienced this with a branded credit card. The credit card company's customer reps treated me so poorly that I canceled my credit card and stopped doing business with the company whose name was on the card. Their business partner lost me as their customer.

Outsourcing

Sometimes it makes sense to outsource work that other companies can do better or cheaper, yet we place our reputation in the hands of someone we have minimal control over. Is it worth the risk?

Conclusion

In these cases, we can succeed or fail based on what our alliance partner does or doesn't do. Though the upside is grand, the downside could negate it all—and more.

Leadership and Management Success Tip

Whether it's sitting on panels, affiliate marketing, strategic alliances, or outsourcing, we must proceed with care, not allowing someone else to control our reputation or our customers.

DO YOU KNOW WHERE YOUR DATA IS?

Corporate Information Is a Critical Asset that Needs Protection

I t doesn't matter what type of company you run, your operation amasses a great deal of valuable data. You have a treasure of customer information, including phone numbers, mailing and email addresses, billing histories, demographic profiles, social security numbers, bank account numbers, and credit card numbers. You purchased some of this data, while you garnered the rest over time, using meticulous recordkeeping.

Even the smallest of businesses possess an

extraordinary amount of priceless information, while larger organizations store millions or billions of data points—all nicely organized, carefully stored, and dutifully backed up.

You have all that information, but what are you doing with it?

No, I'm not talking about harnessing metadata to produce a competitive advantage or turning raw information into a core distinctive. I'm sure you know you must do these things and are working on them. What I am referring to is protecting your immense information stash from the reach of hackers, cyberspace's criminal elite—hard to catch and harder still to prosecute.

With the theft of personal information steadily increasing—due to an insatiable demand and minimal risk—there is a greater likelihood your business could soon be a victim. So, I implore you to protect one of your organization's most valuable assets.

First, you need someone with the knowledge and experience to secure your computers, network, intranet, and internet access points.

Then, give them the resources needed to do their job. I'm not suggesting you provide an unlimited budget or give them a blank check, but when they say it will cost X dollars to do the job, don't provide half that amount and expect full results. If you cut the funds, some items will remain insecure or be only partially secure. That would be akin to locking the doors of your office but leaving the windows open, or installing a building security system but never connecting it to a monitoring station. Don't handcuff the crime stoppers.

Next, know that many security breaches are inside jobs. Yes, I realize you carefully screen new hires and trust your employees to not steal from you. You should hold your staff in high esteem. The reality, however, is that many cases of data theft involve an insider, whether they are complicit or innocently duped.

To address the employee aspect of the equation, you need your human resources department involved, along with IT and your security officer. Together they can put safeguards in place to restrict access, limit the scope of information available, and provide an electronic log of activity. In addition, provide training on what information staff can give out and under what conditions.

Your data—and your company's future—is on the line. Make sure it's a secure one.

Leadership and Management Success Tip

Your company's data may be your most valuable asset—and the least secure. Take every possible step to keep it safe. It's ultimately your responsibility.

WE'RE ON A MISSION

Get Business Insights from a Movie

A recurring line from the 1980 movie *Blues Brothers* has puzzled me. I'm not sure if I should take offense or find amusement with the protagonist's assertion, "We're on a mission from God."

A Mission Statement

The "mission" of this critically disparaged, yet once-popular, film might be to simply levy mayhem upon the city of Chicago. Yet from the script's perspective, the ambition of Jake and Elwood is to "put the band back together."

As mission statements go, this one lacks sophistication. Yet it's simple, and it's empowering.

When most organizations develop a mission statement, they spend months or even years creating the perfect blend of sentiment, intention, and promise. Once honed, they present it with polished prose. They insert the result in the employee handbook, print it on marketing pieces, and hang it on a plaque in the lobby. Many of these are not mission statements at all, but often amount to nothing more than thinly disguised marketing.

An effective mission statement has three important characteristics:

1. Those it applies to need to understand it.
2. It provides direction for daily decision-making.
3. It must be concise, so all stakeholders can learn it, follow it, and internalize it.

Unfortunately, most organizations' mission statements don't fit any of these criteria. The Blues Brothers' mission does. Each time they share it, everyone understands it, has direction, and finds it easy to learn, follow, and internalize.

Supporting Vision

Their mission to put the band back together seems trivial, but behind every mission, there is a supporting vision. The vision of the Blues Brothers is to raise money to save the orphanage that raised them and is now struggling with a lack of funds.

This vision is why their mission is so important. The mission is not the end, but rather a means to the end: saving the orphanage.

Action Steps

Mission and vision, however, aren't enough. Just as the mission finds support from vision, vision deployment occurs through action. The action steps of the Blues Brothers are simple: contact former and prospective band members, get them to join the group, hold a benefit concert, and give the money to the orphanage.

Therefore, the Blues Brothers' business plan looks like this:

Mission: Put the band back together

Vision: Save the orphanage

Action Items:

- Contact musicians
- Restart group
- Hold concert
- Give proceeds to orphanage

Application

Now it's time for introspection.

Does your organization have a mission? A vision? What are your action items?

If you don't have a mission statement, now's the time to develop one. Start today. Don't delay. Make sure your mission statement gives your staff direction. Don't let them flounder. Remember the wise saying, "Where there is no vision, the people perish."

If you already have a mission statement, is it the hang-on-the-wall, marketing-ploy type or the succinctly worded axiom that directs daily actions and guides decisions?

Maybe your stated purpose is a real mission statement. If so, is it short enough for your staff to learn, follow, and internalize? Is it readily understood? Does it serve as a guide for daily decisions and actions?

The conventional wisdom is that creating a mission and forming a vision is a group activity, something done by committee, with input and review throughout the organization. This gets the buy-in of all stakeholders. Yet the reality is that a mission developed this way becomes less relevant as turnover occurs. After a few years, the statement becomes increasingly meaningless. Then a new committee meets to create a different declaration.

This approach is wrong.

Those who helped craft it move on and those who replaced them have no connection with it. Yes, you need to have the support of stakeholders for your mission, but its origin must be from leadership. Therefore, to be of lasting value, the mission must come from the top.

Then communicate this guiding plan not once, not sometimes, but often. Over time, those it's intended to support will grow to embrace it. Only then will it become understood and internalized.

Coming from leadership and supported by management, it will permeate the organization, directing actions and guiding decisions. With this as the expected outcome, make your mission statement your top priority. Your future may be at stake.

Leadership and Management Success Tip

Mission and vision come from the top, not from a committee.

FIVE TIPS FOR SUCCESSFUL DELEGATION

Discover How to Tap Your Employees for Better Results

Many years ago, as a first-time manager, I was green, with much to learn. Management looked easy from the outside. I had assured myself that, when given the opportunity to lead, I'd never make the same blunders I endured.

Yes, I would direct my future staff with enlightenment, never forgetting the negative examples I had witnessed over the years. I pledged to do a better job as a manager. It was a commendable yet lofty goal. But I found it easier to say than do.

One day I trod down the hall, trailing behind my

boss. He had just given me one more assignment, a task I didn't have time for.

I protested, insisting I already had too much on my plate.

"Don't worry," he said. "Just delegate it."

I mentally reviewed the capabilities of my charges. Although they were a group of able young technologists, none were ready for a project of this magnitude or to meet my boss's standards.

"But there's no one I can delegate it to."

"Do you want to know the secret of delegation?" His eyes twinkled.

I edged closer, expecting the secret of managerial nirvana. I nodded.

"It's simple. Just look for your busiest guy and give the project to him!"

His *insight* dumbfounded me. I said nothing, and he continued.

"The busiest guy is the one who gets things done. That's always who you want to delegate to."

Seething, I kept quiet. I flashed a comprehending look, a respectful nod, and a faint smile. His dissemination of knowledge now complete, he strode down the hall, while I ducked into my office and closed the door.

His words angered me on multiple levels.

First, I had yet another project to do. Second, his advice was unfair. Delegating to the busiest employee would only make him or her busier, setting them up to be the leading candidate for the next project. Last, I realized that, as the busiest of those under his command, I was his go-to guy.

There had to be a better way.

It took a while, some research, and lots of trial and error, but I eventually understood the art of delegating. Delegation is something all managers need to do. Unfortunately, it's also hard. Many who attempt it are unhappy with the results, often accepting subpar outcomes or giving up. Sadly, successful delegation requires an initial investment of time, often more time than it would take to do the work yourself.

If that's the case, why bother? It's simply because once you teach your employees how to receive and complete delegated tasks, you'll realize a huge time savings as you empower them, allowing them to grow as individuals and to contribute to your organization's success. As such, delegation is well worth the extra effort to do it right.

A five-step procedure paves the way to successful delegation.

1. Select the Right People

A person who has proven themselves in smaller tasks can handle more responsibilities and enjoy greater latitude. However, until they prove their ability to effectively handle assignments, the scope of their tasks must remain small. For example, if they can't arrive at work on time, is there any reason to assume they can accomplish something more challenging?

To give unproven employees a chance to prove themselves, start with small assignments such as sorting mail, stuffing envelopes, making copies, or simply arriving at work on time. Next, they can graduate to processing shipments or placing an office supply order (you select the items and quantities; they place it).

Each time they successfully complete a delegated assignment, reward them with additional responsibilities. And each time they fail to complete a task, confront them. Train all employees to handle basic delegated projects. If they can't, why are you still employing them? Some employees will advance to assignments of medium difficulty, while a few superstars can work independently. Therefore, match the task to the employee.

2. Ensure They Have the Proper Tools and Knowledge to Do the Job

If the work requires a computer, is one available? If it requires a program, do they know how to use it? Do they have the needed login credentials? Also, consider whether they have the background knowledge to complete the task.

It's easy to oversimplify a project or assume key details are common knowledge. Often, an employee needs instruction or training before they can successfully complete an assignment.

Not only must you ensure you've given them this information but also provide it in the ideal format for them. Some people learn best in written form, others need a demonstration, and some need to actually do it. Occasionally a combination is appropriate.

Regardless, asking an employee to start a project without the proper resources is setting them up to fail.

3. Give Them a Clear Timetable

Saying a project is "urgent" means different things to different people. Telling them, "When you have time," is open to misinterpretation. When giving a deadline, you cannot be too specific. Examples include, "I require your written overview on my desk every Monday by 5 p.m.," or "I need your preliminary work by the end of the day on Thursday, the twelfth."

4. Hold Them Accountable

Follow-up must be consistent and expected. Let them know you'll check on their progress. Assure them you're available for questions.

If they do unsatisfactory work or miss a deadline, there must be a reaction. This could be merely asking them to explain what happened. Perhaps, despite your best efforts, the instructions were incomplete, or training was insufficient. Then shoulder the blame and correct the oversight.

Sometimes, managers need to communicate the ramifications, such as, "Because you did not complete this on time, we lost the client, which will cost us X dollars." If you correctly follow step one, only rare cases will need disciplinary action.

5. Give Them Bigger Assignments as They Prove Themselves

Now you can phase out of step 4, accountability. Yes, accountability must remain, but it gradually becomes ancillary to delegation, instead of integral.

Conclusion

If you consistently follow these steps, all employees will become better at responding to delegation. Some staff will advance to the point of self-determination, where they take the initiative to do needed work.

That is delegation at its finest.

Leadership and Management Success Tip

Spending time training your staff to handle delegated projects is an investment that will have a huge return.

COUNTING CHICKENS

Lessons in Managing Employees

In my office hangs an evocative black-and-white aerial photo of my grandfather's chicken farm, circa 1960. He and Dad ran the operation, along with a revolving assortment of hired help. The farm comprised five barns, in two interconnected groups. Together they accommodated 15,000 hens.

As a preschooler, I would sometimes get to go with Dad to help gather eggs. It was great fun—for the first few minutes. I quickly learned to avoid nests with hens in them. They would peck the back of your hand. Even the jersey gloves with cut-off fingers that Dad wore provided inadequate protection. I resorted to gathering eggs from empty nests, in the lower rows I could reach. Once I needed to rest and sat on a little stool. Only it wasn't a stool. It was a basket of eggs. I broke half of them before I could wriggle out of it. I was mortified. Dad patiently cleaned me off. Grandpa laughed.

Unfortunately, because of health issues for Dad and a sudden desire by Grandpa to retire, Grandpa closed the farm and sold the hens. The next day, as I took my usual shortcut to school through the back of the farm, I spotted a wayward hen who had escaped deportation. My cousin Steve and I tried in vain to catch her. I knew we needed expert help and ran to get Grandpa. Although skeptical of my tale, he went to help. Alas, we found neither chicken nor Steve. Grandpa suggested I get to school, and I later learned that Steve had caught the skittish hen. At a loss of what to do, he put her in the cab of Grandpa's old dump truck.

"Can I keep it?" I begged Mom and Dad. Dad couldn't say no. My hen garnered me a private supply of eggs, producing one every 27 hours. (The exact laying cycle varies with breed, age, diet, environment, and season.) This was short of my hope for an egg a day, so I considered a second hen.

That would be more eggs than I needed, so I would share with my family. *Why stop at two?* my young mind reasoned. Six hens would produce enough for everyone, with some left over. A dozen hens would mean eggs to sell. How far could it grow? Soon my elementary-school entrepreneurialism envisioned me helping feed and support my family.

I'm not sure if I shared this great vision with Dad, but when I asked for a second hen, he agreed. Dad picked a robust layer. She was a fine specimen, and I was ecstatic.

Unfortunately, my two hens didn't get along, with the new one dominating and attacking the original. Even with a larger pen, the abuse continued, production dropped, and soon my cherished pet was dead, killed by her associate and my desire for more. That day, my dream died too.

But this isn't a story about chickens. It's about people. It's not a commentary on greed or a rant against capitalism, but rather a call for balance and pragmatism:

Bigger Is Not Always Better

Sometimes the adage is true that less is more. Enough said.

Increased Scope Produces Increased Challenges

I was a successful farmer of one chicken. But I wrongly assumed that if I could raise one, two would not be a problem because it's a scalable concept. I never dreamed that I would have *labor* issues to deal with. It never came up in a one-chicken operation.

All too often, businesspeople expand their operation without considering the ramifications. They forget that a bigger operation requires more support and adds unforeseen challenges. This often occurs when a successful, one-location business opens a second site. Suddenly, neither does well. It might be that the owners have the wrong management style, they become distracted, or they lack requisite infrastructure.

Value What You Have

I took my hen for granted. When a better one came along, I jumped at the opportunity.

I've done the same with employees. Maybe you have too.

You have people whose work may not be stellar, but who have been steady, faithful, and dependable for years. Then a bright-eyed, eager-to-please applicant arrives and the next thing you know, the new employee has chased the proven one away.

It's only then that you realize the newer model wasn't the solution you expected. You long for the good ole days with your trusty assistant, before things got messed up with a new hire and your longing for something better.

Personal Application

We live in a society that is seldom satiated and always lusts for more. It's not bad to have dreams and set goals. In fact, it's good to do so, and it's detrimental to lack aspirations. Yet when the push for more becomes the focus, the best parts of life can become obscured, going unnoticed and unrealized.

The first step is to truly distinguish between needs and wants. So many things that we think we need are unnecessary and merely a nice extra. How important is a bigger house, a newer car, a grander vacation, or more "toys"? Will they bring joy and satisfaction or just make you more tired, with added pressures?

Ask yourself, "When was the last time I wore out an article of clothing, as opposed to merely getting bored with it or it becoming too tight?" This gets to the crux of the issue. Being content with what we have is a good place to strive for. Learning to be satisfied with less is even better—and will still leave us ahead of most people on the planet.

Don't get so busy counting your chickens that you lose sight of what you have.

Leadership and Management Success Tip

Don't assume that scaling up an operation is easy. Make sure you're ready to deal with the increased problems that bigger will bring.

IT'S ALL VIRTUAL

Discover the Benefits of Having a Virtual Company

As I contemplated my periodical publishing business, circa 2006, the realization struck me that I had a virtual company. This wasn't intentional. It just worked out that way. I was the only one working in the "corporate office." Everyone who took part in the production of the magazines lived in different states. There were no local vendors either.

As editor, I planned, solicited, and edited the articles and press releases. A copy editor/proofreader polished the content. She lived in Connecticut.

My media rep was in New York. She handled the display advertising sales, receiving digital artwork, which she forwarded to my graphic designer. He was in Pennsylvania. He uploaded the files to our printer in Ohio. The printer worked up the proofs, which they posted on a private server for us to approve.

I handled the mailing list, which I emailed to our list processor. They cleaned up the data and sorted the addresses, which they forwarded to our printer. The printer merged the mailing list with the magazines and transported them to the post office. An army of postal carriers delivered the finished product across the country.

We conducted business via telephone and frequently used email. We produced each issue with no face-to-face interaction. At first this was disconcerting, but I'm convinced the result was better than if we had all worked together in the same office.

True, we missed some synergy, incidental communication, and camaraderie, but we were also free to do what each of us did best and to do so with minimal distraction and interruption.

Since that time, I've tapped designers, consultants, and assistants from around the world. They hail from Canada, the United Kingdom, Romania, India, the Philippines, and Australia, as well as the

United States. This effectively makes my company of one person also an international one.

None of these fine people are employees. They're all independent contractors. This gives me options to meet business needs in an efficient and cost-effective way. And it gives them flexibility in their work, producing multiple streams of income due to having multiple clients, and allowing the potential for a better work-life balance.

I also work in a virtual office. It's a spare bedroom in my home. I've done this since 2000, long before it was common.

As a virtual business with a virtual office and virtual staff, I save on overhead expenses and have a nimble, responsive company.

It's all virtual, and it's all good.

Leadership and Management Success Tip

Consider how your company can benefit by going virtual—or to move in that direction.

OUTSOURCING

An Option to Save Money, Improve Quality, and Increase Profits

L
ike my business, some organizations could similarly configure themselves as a virtual operation. Not all, however, are ready. An option that falls between a traditional business model and a virtual operation is outsourcing.

Increasingly, businesses outsource some aspects of their work. Though this may be to individuals—as I do with my virtual operation—tapping other companies to assist is more common. One business outsources work to another.

It's important to note that *outsource* doesn't imply another country. Despite media attention to the contrary, most outsourcing occurs to businesses *within* the same country.

Outsourcing Options

Conventional wisdom says you don't outsource your core competencies. But what if someone else can do it better or cheaper? What if your labor market has an effective zero percent unemployment rate or you want to get off the continuous hiring treadmill?

These are all reasons to consider outsourcing.

Most organizations have six functional areas: operations, customer service, sales and marketing, technical, accounting, and management. I've yet to see one company do all six with excellence, yet any viable concern shines in at least one area. Even the strong players master only three or four.

Since no one excels at everything, it's practical to consider outsourcing the weak areas of your company. Then you can focus on what you do best, and your company will perform better as a result. You, too, could even become a virtual company of one, like me.

Outsourcing Selection

As you look for outsourcing partners, take care in your selection. A wrong choice could be costly or even crippling, but you can also quickly correct the situation by merely finding a new firm to handle that aspect of your business.

When outsourcing large functions, you may want to avoid putting "all your eggs in one basket," dividing the work between multiple vendors. This increases flexibility and minimizes risk.

You should scrutinize an outsourcing partner just like you would any other vendor. "Look before you leap." Referrals are valuable. Check references. Visit them in person. Ask questions—both to them and of yourself.

What does their facility look like? Are they big enough to handle your work? Are they small enough to care about your account? Do you have respect for the key people in their company? Is there potential for a long-term business relationship?

Last, find out who will be your primary contact on a day-to-day basis. How well do you mesh with that person? What is their anticipated future with the company? Should this contact leave, will your satisfaction with the outsourcer's service disappear as well, or will someone else be capable of taking over without negatively impacting your organization?

Don't enter any outsourcing agreement lightly or without due diligence. But when properly executed for the right reasons, the results can be both liberating and profitable.

Leadership and Management Success Tip

Consider areas you can outsource to other companies. Also explore if your company can provide outsourcing services to others.

A SOLOPRENEUR

Leading and Managing a Staff of Subcontractors and Freelancers

For the past several years I've been a solopreneur. That is, I'm a company of one. Initially I offered consultancy services. Then I added periodical publishing to the mix and phased out the consulting work. I later added commercial freelance writing, while authoring and publishing books. My latest iteration focuses entirely on books.

When you oversee a company of one, many assume that leadership and management become a non-issue. But I assure you, this is not true.

Lead and Manage Yourself

Though it may at first seem strange to say, it's critical to lead and manage yourself. This is even more important as a solopreneur than as an entrepreneur or businessperson.

Working on your own requires self-discipline. It demands sacrifice. There's the ever-present reality that if I don't do it, it doesn't happen. And if I procrastinate, I won't complete my work on time. And when disaster strikes, I—and I alone—am responsible to handle it. There's no one else to help. Therefore, it's critical to lead ourselves well and manage our work with excellence.

This idea of leading and managing self, however, doesn't just apply to the solopreneur. Wise leaders and managers realize the need to lead and manage themselves too. This is regardless of the size of the organization or the role they're in.

No one will take care of ourselves like we can. That's why it's critical to do just that. With intention, we must lead and manage ourselves every day.

Lead and Manage Subcontractors

Though a solopreneur has no employees, they tap into array of independent specialists, freelancers, and subcontractors. For the sake of simplicity, we'll call them all subcontractors.

As a solopreneur, I've always relied on a group of carefully vetted subcontractors to handle areas I'm not skilled at or don't have time to complete. This has varied over the years but, at any given time, I've always had about a half dozen subcontractors providing services for me that I can't do myself. They hail from around the world, often working when I'm not. For some, English is a secondary language, which requires careful communication to avoid misunderstandings.

Though some have worked on single projects and others for a season, most perform ongoing tasks. Once I accepted the idea of tapping subcontractors as opposed to hiring staff, I readily embraced the idea.

When a 40-hour-a-week employee leaves, you're suddenly confronted with forty hours of work you need to figure out how to deal with. The solutions vary between hiring a replacement, delegating aspects of the job to other employees, or doing the work yourself. Occasionally you realize that some of that former employee's work is nonessential and not needed for the ongoing viability of the business.

Therefore, it's safe to discontinue some of that person's work.

In contrast, when the subcontractor leaves, it's one defined task to deal with. It's usually a straightforward process to find another subcontractor with that skill set.

Yet to be effective, you must lead and manage these subcontractors. In some ways, leading and managing dispersed workers who are not on the payroll is harder than managing those who are.

I only ever met one of my subcontractors in person. And only a few have I interacted with through video conferencing. Most exist by name only behind the veil of an email or app.

It might be easy to dismiss subcontractors as a commodity and treat them poorly because they're easy to replace. But this is a shortsighted perspective.

Treat them with respect, and they'll be more apt to respect you. Give them your loyalty, and they'll be more disposed to be loyal to you. Be fair to them, and they'll be more prone to be fair to you. Do more than expected for them, and they'll often do more than expected for you.

Just as it's easy to end a relationship with a subcontractor, it's also easy for a subcontractor to end their work with you. This is especially true if their skills are in demand. When this is the case, they replace demanding or low-paying clients with those who are easier to work with or pay better.

Because of this, I work to foster good working relationships with all my subcontractors. I strive to be understanding, patient, and accommodating—sometimes to a fault—so they can realize a better work-life balance and achieve their goals.

Though I have had to let some virtual assistants go because of performance issues, I've never ended a work relationship with any of my other subcontractors. Our work arrangement ends by their choice when their focus, priorities, or needs change. As far as I know, we've always parted on good terms.

Though I've always strived to have good working relationships with employees, it's also important to lead and manage subcontractors well.

Leadership and Management Success Tip

Don't overlook caring for your subcontractors—or yourself. Success depends on it.

THEY JUST DON'T GET IT

*When the Business Model that Once Worked No
Longer Does*

Back when I had a local phone company, I
wondered if they were clueless. They just
didn't get it. By *it*, I mean everything:
marketing, pricing, retention, technical support, and
customer service.

Although they were surely aware that they no
longer functioned in a monopoly environment, their
actions belied that reality.

Consider:

Marketing

My phone company would send me direct mail and bill stuffers. Since I'd been their customer for twenty-two years, they should know me, making offers applicable to my service.

Alas, they did not. They once delighted me when a bill stuffer offered DSL service for only $17 a month, guaranteed to *never* go up. That was half what I currently paid, so I immediately called. The rep was engaging and helpful—until she learned I already had DSL service.

She explained that this offer was for new customers only. I didn't qualify.

I understand the allure of offering promotional rates to snag new business, but doing so disrespects longstanding customers. It's even worse to flaunt it by sending that enticing offer to someone who is already paying twice as much—and then refusing to lower their rate.

She apologized for the error.

Bundling

I expressed my desire to lower my bill. She offered me several packages: DSL and long distance, DSL and local calling, DSL and satellite

TV, and the triple play: DSL, cell phone, and satellite TV. In each instance, I would need to make a long-term commitment. And my bill would *increase.*

None of the packages made sense.

Long ago, my phone company had inadvertently trained me to not make long-distance calls on my landline, opting to use my cell phone instead with its free long distance. My satellite service and cell phone are with competing companies that charge less.

She tried to get me to switch. I didn't budge.

Customer Retention

Just the month before, I had slashed the cost of my business service 40 percent just by asking them to lower my bill. I'm not sure what the rep did, but she made it happen. As a result, my business line became a fraction of the cost of my residential service. Surely, my residential service could likewise be lower.

I pleaded with her for a way to reduce my rate. Not making any progress, I asked if I could cancel my local number and keep my DSL. Yes, that was possible, but the cost of the DSL would increase by

50 percent—and be almost *three times* their promotional offer.

Sensing that my entire account might be in jeopardy, she offered to change my "unlimited" local dialing plan to "economy." Then I'd pay four cents for each local call, but at my limited usage, it would have saved me several dollars a month.

However, we could merely make those local calls from our cell phones, saving even more. Once again, they motivated me to bypass their network.

Technical Support

When we first had DSL service, I'd report problems as soon as they occurred. The response of the technical staff shocked me. They would assume it was my problem and that their equipment wasn't at fault. They'd have me changing the configuration on my computers and network, moving cables, and effectively migrating to an unworkable condition.

Then they would reluctantly admit that the problem was not mine but theirs. They would promise a twenty-four-hour response time and hang up, leaving me to put things back to normal.

I eventually learned to *not* call to report outages but to take a break instead, as the issues tended to be resolved within an hour or two without me doing anything. One time, however, there was an exception to this pattern.

Customer Service

We lost our DSL service one Saturday evening. It was late anyway, so we stopped working for the day. On Sunday morning it was still down, and it was still out that afternoon too. I reported the problem that evening, expecting it would work again by Monday morning.

Submitting the trouble ticket was an arduous task, with multiple levels of menus to navigate, sparring with uncooperative speech recognition software, and entering and verifying my phone number.

What was most exacerbating, however, is that *after* I pressed the option indicating I couldn't connect to the internet, their recording kept referring me to online tech support for faster service. Of course, once I finally reached a person, the first thing they did was ask for my phone number, which I'd already entered.

Initially, the tech said the problem was on my end, but he later changed his mind, claiming that a repairperson would need to be sent on site.

Someone would call me on Monday between 8:00 a.m. and 5:00 p.m. To my shock, he warned me that *if I didn't answer when they called, they'd cancel the trouble ticket and bill me.*

I never left the phone on Monday, and they never called. On my second attempt that day to reach them, I got through, asking what happened to their promised 5:00 p.m. repair commitment.

The agent apologized, testing the line again. She wondered if a remote fix would work. She told me I'd receive an automated call once they resolved the problem. This would be on Tuesday.

Knowing to not believe anything they said, I tested the internet later that evening, and it worked. The automated call, however, didn't come until the next day.

Conclusion

Lest you assume this is an outdated situation. It is not. Though I've not had local phone service for over a decade, my mother still does. And they still play the same games with her.

Her local phone company just doesn't get it—but I'm sure *you* do.

Leadership and Management Success Tip

Consider how business models and customer expectations have changed. Look for what needs an update—or overhaul—in your business. Opportunities for improvement await, if only you will seek them.

BEAM ME UP, SCOTTY

Leadership Lessons from Star Trek

It was a lazy summer afternoon. Things were slow at the office and upper management had all left to get an early jump on their weekend. I, being a mid-level manager, didn't have that luxury. Besides, I still had work to do.

My first clue that something was amiss came from increased activity in the hallway outside my office. There was more movement than usual. People were running. Snickering and subdued shrieking replace reserved talk and business-appropriate laughter. An impromptu game of tag had materialized.

Concerned that my staff was involved, I went to check. To my relief, the culprits were from a different department. Even so, my stern glare sent them scurrying.

I didn't know if they merely retreated to friendlier confines or if common sense overcame them. Regardless, they left my area, and I returned to my office.

Several minutes later, the next instance of impropriety came via the overhead paging system. They paged a rookie to call an extension, which I recognized as a non-existent number. I smiled, envisioning a frustrated greenhorn dutifully dialing a number that didn't work. Certainly, the conspirators were watching from some hidden vantage point, gleefully snickering.

This was repeated a few times, and when their victim realized their scheme and stopped responding, they paged him with the legitimate extension of a secretary who would have no tolerance for their tomfoolery.

Wise to their prank, the resourceful trainee reciprocated with a page of his own. This soon escalated to a "paging" war, drawing in more people, with increasingly ridiculous announcements.

A final page stopped the misfits in their tracks. In

a reasonable impersonation of Captain Kirk, one employee accessed the overhead paging system and, with all seriousness, intoned, "Beam me up, Scotty. There's no intelligent life down here."

I stopped working, smiled, and then laughed. Noticing it was now after five, I got up, turned off the lights, and went home. Work could wait.

Star Trek Captains

I've had a long fascination with *Star Trek*. Many societal problems are resolved or minimized in the future according to *Star Trek*, providing a mostly utopian existence where evil usually resides outside the Federation. *Star Trek* also has a realistic underlying basis in scientific fact, albeit stretched thin at times—the transporters are the biggest scientific leap. In addition, with good plots and cleverly intertwined story lines, it makes for good drama.

It isn't optimism for the future, realistic scientific stories, or compelling plots, however, that give me the most pause for consideration. Rather, it's the lessons *Star Trek* provides in leadership.

Entertainment value aside, I embrace *Star Trek* as a study in effectively leading people and managing staff. What lessons can we learn from the *Star Trek* captains? How do they elicit such devotion and dedication among their crews?

Demonstrate Loyalty

Although Starfleet personnel are trained to obey their leaders, the crews show loyalty to their captains. Why? Because the captains first show loyalty to them.

This loyalty is earned, not demanded. Each captain makes excessive efforts and takes extreme risks for an injured, wayward, or stranded crew member.

When leaders put everything on the line for a follower, the follower is much more inclined to do the same for the leader and to more fully embrace their common cause.

Shoulder Blame and Share Credit

A true side of leadership is to shoulder the blame for an erring, but otherwise worthy, subordinate, while being sure to shower accolades on those who deserve it. This is what *Star Trek* captains do. So should we.

Conversely, selfish leaders seek to make themselves look good by assigning blame to others and taking credit for what they did not do.

Tap into Expertise

Starfleet captains often put together ad hoc teams for specific missions, mixing senior officers with junior members who possess a unique skill or training. This provides junior staff with a terrific opportunity to rise to the occasion, performing at a higher level and with increased confidence, which bolsters their value to the crew, the captain, and Starfleet.

Once employees prove themselves in this way, you can groom them for greater responsibility. They are promotable.

Celebrate Unconventional Thinking

A recurring theme in many *Star Trek* episodes finds the crew confronting an unstoppable impending disaster. There appears to be no escape and no plausible solution. Yet one of the crew members, in a moment of creative insight, extraordinary deduction, or brilliant intuition finds a unique solution and saves the entire crew.

Star Trek captains delight in this and so do effective leaders. In addition, as you reward and recognize unconventional solutions, you reinforce and encourage innovative behavior.

Simply stated, influential leaders inspire their charges to innovate.

Be Worthy of Imitation

Each captain and every effective leader possesses admirable qualities, worthy of emulation. These positive traits draw both crew and staff to their leaders, compelling them to imitate the example they see.

When leaders have no one following them, it hints that they're not admirable enough to follow.

Get Real

Each captain is tough when he or she needs to be. They also have a human side, however, that those in their inner circle witness. This provides a connection that transcends rough spots in relationships and times of stress.

A Final Consideration

It took me too long to realize the ultimate reason why Starfleet captains are such successful leaders. The answer is simple: that's how the writers made them.

Even so, we can learn valuable leadership lessons from the *Star Trek* captains.

Leadership and Management Success Tip

Pick a leadership lesson that you need to implement or improve.

GIVE BACK TO YOUR COMMUNITY

Though Our Goal Is to Make Money, It Shouldn't Be Our Only Motivation

Working in any business is challenging and demanding. Leading and managing one is even harder. Daily activity seems, all too often, to consist of reacting to the urgency of the moment. There is little time to plan and few opportunities to look beyond the confines of the company walls.

Yet looking beyond is exactly what you need to do. Seeking ways to give back to your community may be precisely the action you should pursue.

Some organizations have done so with profound results.

Why Give?

There are many reasons why it's wise for a business to give back to its community. Aside from principled reasons, the practical justification is that it's good for business. Community involvement expands networking opportunities, increases corporate standing, and generates goodwill.

From an employee standpoint, it builds camaraderie as staffers serve together and pursue common non-work-related goals, increases employer esteem, and provides a connection outside the workplace. These have an indirect effect of improving employee job satisfaction and decreasing turnover. Last, as employees see a different side to their employer, respect can increase and better understanding can be nurtured.

With all these benefits, what company wouldn't want to promote and pursue a philanthropic effort?

What to Give?

You can provide two primary forms of aid: labor

and money. Most nonprofits are more in need of volunteer labor than they are of monetary donations. (As nonprofits find volunteers scarcer, however, they need funds to hire the labor that was once volunteered.)

Labor: Let's start with the labor aspect. You can provide opportunities for your staff to volunteer. They can go in groups. It's easier to go somewhere new or try something different if it happens with a friend. In addition, there's the bonus of being able to serve together. This has its own reward. Generally, these opportunities should occur outside regular working hours.

Some businesses have a provision to take time off without pay. A few even offer paid time off when volunteering. These, however, are rare, costly to the company, and not needed. Setting up a simple means to allow employees to know about and pursue volunteer opportunities takes little time and incurs little cost.

Money: For many people it's easier to write a check than to volunteer. The same is true for businesses. If a corporate financial donation isn't an option, don't worry about it. Having you and your staff involved is more important anyway.

If you can make a financial contribution,

consider setting up a matching fund program. This is when companies budget monies to match the donations of their employees. The employee makes the donation, submits the receipt, and the company makes a matching contribution.

This, too, is quite easy to set up. Payroll deductions for charities are also an option, but more costly and time-consuming to implement. Of course, there is also the option for the business to make a direct contribution.

Where to Give?

Needs exist all around your community. Find out what is already going on. Consider after-school programs, food pantries, clothes closets, homeless shelters, and soup kitchens. Call your nearest school and ask how you can help. Opportunities might include adopt-a-classroom, reading programs, tutoring, mentoring, or providing back-to-school supplies.

If you have a college nearby, check with the service organizations on campus and see how you can support them. A side benefit of working with college students is that you will interact with potential job candidates. Just make sure that employee prospecting doesn't become the reason for getting involved.

Who to Give To?

I hope your mind is now spinning with ideas. So many needs, so many opportunities, so much to do. It can quickly overwhelm. Being overwhelmed leads to discouragement, which leads to inaction. The key to prevent this from occurring is to whittle down the list, identify one organization that's a good fit, and focus on how *you* can help *them.*

Just one.

Ask your employees for recommendations. They'll suggest groups that they already support with their time or money. Although only a small percentage of your staff will currently be involved with any organization, it's an ideal place to start. They already have a connection and an affiliation. They can acclimate others as they step forward to volunteer.

You will also have some staffers who have esteem for a particular organization but have not yet taken that first step toward involvement. Those recommendations are also worth considering. Again, their predilection for that organization will help move things forward.

Before you make a final selection, investigate the organization just as you would for an important business purchase or partnership:

- Find out how long they have been in your community.
- Review their annual report.
- Ask what percentage of donations goes to overhead.
- See if the Better Business Bureau has a file on them or what the Chamber of Commerce may know.

If these all look good, meet with the executive director, ask to attend a board meeting, and seek a straightforward way to test if you are a good fit for each other.

Regardless of the size of your business, pick just one organization to support—at least initially. It's far better to make a significant and sustained effort to one group than to spread resources thinly across many organizations. This results in ineffectiveness.

Once you have successfully proven your company can support one organization, then you may consider a second one, but proceed slowly and with care. Remember that for many companies, especially smaller ones, focusing on one group is ideal.

How to Give?

Once you select a group to work with and identify an initial area of focus, it's time to act. Ideally, company leaders should be in this first wave of volunteering, setting an example and inspiring others to follow. As previously mentioned, it's easier to go as a group, especially for the first few times.

Hopefully, there are already one or more employees who have practical volunteer experience with the organization. Let them take a lead role, comfortably easing others in and leading by example. In no time, everyone will serve with practiced confidence. Then they can repeat the process with others.

It's important to remember that, no matter how great the need or how rewarding the work, only a percentage of employees will take part. Also, their involvement will vary. Expect this and accept it.

Make sure no one feels obligated to get involved, and remind them that volunteering is, in fact, voluntary. You don't want to serve with someone who is negative. The goal is to have fun and find fulfillment as you volunteer. Leave the naysayers at the office.

When to Give?

Now! Not next year, not next month. Right now.

Leadership and Management Success Tip

Extend your leadership into your community to help others and give back. Not only will this benefit everyone involved, it's also the right thing to do.

MOVING FORWARD

Lead with Integrity and Manage with Confidence

I've spent much of my career leading and managing people. The result has been rewarding and most fulfilling. I have many happy memories of the talented people I've worked with and the challenges we faced together, successfully navigating them as a team. These are experiences I cherish.

Yet I have not been without my share of missteps along the way. Such is the case for every leader and manager. What's critical is that we learn from our mistakes and take steps to not repeat them.

Even better is when we can learn from others to

avoid committing blunders in the first place. Likewise, we can learn to emulate their successes.

That's the goal of this book. My hope is that
you'll take these lessons and move forward with
greater effectiveness to lead and manage well. As
you do, those under you will benefit, as will your
organization.

Embedded throughout these pages is an underlying theme of integrity. I don't share my experiences
and these examples so that you can earn more
money or achieve greater success. Those outcomes
are ancillary. I write to encourage you to lead and
manage well and do so with the confidence that your
priorities point in the right direction.

To move forward, review the leadership and
success tips at the end of each chapter. Note which
ones resonate with you. Let this list inform your
action plan. Now pick the top three that are easier to
implement, while producing meaningful results.
Last, determine which of the three deserves your
greatest attention today.

Turn them into your goals for the rest of this
year. Don't put this off until January 1 rolls around.
Start today.

Let your top leadership and management goal be
your primary focus. Use the second and third ones

to round out your personal initiatives to lead and manage with more effectiveness. Commit to achieving them. Set a timetable.

Chart your progress throughout the year. Commit to making incremental improvements, and you will end the year in a much better place than where you started. Your staff will thank you.

Continue this process each year, picking new leadership and management success tips to guide your path forward.

Leading and managing people is both challenging and rewarding. Not everyone can do it. And even fewer can do it well. But if you made it this far in the book, I suspect you're someone with the drive and potential to lead and manage others with excellence.

As a last action item, consider who you want to help to be a better leader and manager. Give them a copy of this book so they can learn its lessons too. Go through it with them or even form a discussion group with your inner circle.

As you do so, remember that this book is just a tool to help you succeed. The outcome depends on you. Now make it happen.

You can do it!

OTHER BOOKS IN THE STICKY SERIES

Which book in the Sticky Series do you want to read next?

Sticky Customer Service: Stop Churning Customers and Start Growing Your Business

Sticky Sales and Marketing: Produce Positive Long-Term Results and Relationships

Sticky Living: Live a Life that Matters to Your Family, Friends, and Community

ABOUT PETER LYLE DEHAAN

Peter Lyle DeHaan is an entrepreneur and businessman who has managed, owned, or started multiple businesses over his career. Common themes at every turn have included leadership and management, customer service, and sales and marketing. He shares his lifetime of business experience and personal insights with others through his books and blog posts to encourage, inspire, and occasionally entertain.

Learn more at peterlyledehaan.com.

If you liked *Sticky Leadership and Management*, please leave a review online. Your review will help others discover this book and encourage them to read it too.

Thank you.

OTHER BOOKS BY PETER LYLE DEHAAN

Sticky Series

Sticky Customer Service

Sticky Sales and Marketing

Sticky Living

Call Center Success Series

Healthcare Call Center Essentials

How to Start a Telephone Answering Service

Other Books

Successful Author FAQs

Academic Research

The Telephone Answering Service Industry

Turning a Telephone Answering Service into a Call Center

For the latest list of all Peter Lyle DeHaan's books go to
peterlyledehaan.com/books/.